PENGUIN BOOKS
Amassed Hysteria!

It's a Scream

'Welcome to *Amassed Hysteria!*. For maximum
reading pleasure, please loosen your shoes, kick
out your knees, snap the elastic webbing in your
very best pair of comedy pants and snuggle down
deep.

   'This book that you are holding in your hands is
the actual very same one that you are about to
read: it contains language and scenes that
some of you may find on the following
pages. You can't put a price on that,
can you? Well, *we* managed to put a
price on it, actually, and you paid it.
For that and much else besides, many
thanks' – *Stephen Fry*

The *HYSTERIA!* Guide to Simple, Carefree Shopping: Lesson 1

Out of the kindness of their hearts the kind people at The Hysteria Trust have kindly arranged for *Hysteria 3!*, the video, cassette and CD, to be made available to you. So rush to your local ironmongery, patisserie or haberdashery store and ask for the EMI titles *Hysteria 3!*, the video, *Hysteria 3!*, the cassette, and *Hysteria 3!*, the CD. Then if, and only if, you have enough money, the kind salesperson will kindly sell them to you.

Amassed **H**ysteria!

A COLLECTION OF GREAT COMEDY SKETCHES
FROM *HYSTERIA!*, *HYSTERIA 2!* AND *HYSTERIA 3!*

Directed by Stephen Fry

Compiled by Lise Mayer and Rachel Swann

Written and performed by:
Clive Anderson Rowan Atkinson Morwenna Banks Billy Bragg
Jon Canter John Cleese Alan Cumming Richard Curtis
Adrian Edmondson Ben Elton Harry Enfield Fascinating Aida
Craig Ferguson Dawn French Emma Freud Stephen Fry
Rob Grant Jerry Hall Jeremy Hardy Marie Helvin Lenny Henry
Charles Higson Kit Hollerbach Eddie Izzard Elton John Dillie Keane
Kit and The Widow Hugh Laurie Josie Lawrence Helen Lederer
Robert Llewellyn Chris Lynam Johnny Marr Lise Mayer Mike McShane
Doug Naylor Nigel Planer Vic Reeves Jennifer Saunders
Tony Slattery Tina Turner Richard Vranch Ruby Wax John Wells
Paul Whitehouse Who Dares Wins Steven Wright

Photographers:
Adrian Boot
Johnny Boylan, assisted by Sirie Hills
David Sillitoe (for the *Guardian*)
Alan Sheldon, assisted by Nick Henry
Trevor Leighton

Illustrations:
Nicola Jennings

PENGUIN BOOKS

PENGUIN BOOKS

Published by the Penguin Group
Penguin Books Ltd, 27 Wrights Lane, London w8 5TZ, England
Penguin Books USA Inc., 375 Hudson Street, New York, New York 10014, USA
Penguin Books Australia Ltd, Ringwood, Victoria, Australia
Penguin Books Canada Ltd, 10 Alcorn Avenue, Toronto, Ontario, Canada M4V 3B2
Penguin Books (NZ) Ltd, 182–190 Wairau Road, Auckland 10, New Zealand

Penguin Books Ltd, Registered Offices: Harmondsworth, Middlesex, England

This collection first published 1991
1 3 5 7 9 10 8 6 4 2

The Billy Bragg/Johnny Marr song 'Sexuality' is reprinted by kind permission of
BMG Music Publishing Ltd/Warner Chappell Ltd.

Fascinating Aida's songs ''Allo, Bonjour, Monsieur' and 'Lieder',
from the album *A Load of Old Sequins*, © 1987 Sweet 'n' Sour Songs Ltd,
are reprinted by kind permission of Sweet 'n' Sour Songs Ltd.

The compilers and publishers of this book acknowledge the generosity of the
copyright owners with gratitude.

Printed in England by Clays Ltd, St Ives plc

Contents

Acknowledgements

Thanks to: the Apple Centre, Mortimer Street, London W1; Geoff Atkinson; Channel 4 Stills Department; Penelope Chong; Simon Clark; Fiona Cotter Craig; Sally Debonnaire; Jo Foster; Anthony Goff; Jo Green; Greg Hunt; David Johnson; Crispin Leyser; Camilla Nicholls; Noel Gay Television; Nick Rae; Retna Pictures Ltd; Michelle Rikh; Rajna Sarda; Amanda Swift; the Terrence Higgins Trust; Tiger Television; David Tyler; James Ware; Kate Williams.

Original *Hysteria!* graphic design: Bostock & Pollitt.

The Terrence Higgins Trust

'At the end of the century there could be 10 million people with AIDS. The challenge for the Terrence Higgins Trust now and in the future must be to develop its role as the epidemic changes.'
Virginia Bottomley, Health Minister.

The Terrence Higgins Trust was set up in 1983 to inform, advise and help on all aspects of AIDS and HIV infection. We are the leading UK charity in the fight against AIDS and provide a range of services, 95% of which are provided by trained and committed volunteers.

We aim to meet the ordinary, practical needs, as well as the emotional needs, of women, men and children directly affected by AIDS and HIV, and those who support, love and care for them.

... my eternal gratitude and love for those people at the Terrence Higgins Trust in 1985 when I was first diagnosed HIV positive. Their support and friendship was the lighthouse in a very lonely sea. From that time on, when I did buddy-training and buddied a wonderful guy until his death, (to) my subsequent diagnosis of AIDS – during all that time I was helped and cared for by so many people at the Trust.' *Peter Tilson*

To achieve this we offer a variety of help. We provide counselling, support and advocacy through our Helpline and Legal Line. In addition, we provide face to face counselling, welfare, housing and legal advice. THT operates a hardship fund for those people with AIDS and HIV who are living in the severest poverty and practically we provide one-off assistance with removals, decorating and any similar task of a short term nature.

Probably the most well known of our services is our Buddying Scheme. This innovative project matches people with AIDS with a volunteer who befriends them and offers consistent practical and emotional one-to-one support.

The Terrence Higgins Trust has an extensive health education

The Terrence Higgins Trust

programme, crucial to the raising of public awareness of this health crisis, and act as an information resource to District and Regional Health Authorities.

> 'Over the years the Terrence Higgins Trust, through its members, staff and volunteers, has done an immense amount of good in raising public awareness of HIV infection and has been of great assistance to patients and doctors trying to cope in the stressful circumstances of this disease.' *Leading UK HIV/AIDS Doctors.*

Last year we:

- Provided 385 Buddies
- Responded to 489 requests for practical one-off assistance
- Provided 1,200 counselling sessions
- Took over 15,000 Helpline calls
- Dealt with 1,741 legal issues
- Made 800 small grants
- Archived 2,000 records
- Attended 190 speaking engagements
- Helped with 2,487 welfare rights enquiries
- Gave housing advice to 45% of all newly diagnosed adults

The Terrence Higgins Trust receives limited funding from the Department of Health, Local and Regional Health Authorities and is increasingly dependent upon the support of companies, private donations and charitable trusts.

Benefit concerts such as *Hysteria 3!* play a vital role in not only raising much needed funds for the work of the Terrence Higgins Trust but helping to dispel the misinformation, confusion, ignorance and discrimination that surround HIV and AIDS. We thank all the artists, sponsors, organizers and crew for their support, and above all Stephen Fry for his invaluable contribution to the fight against AIDS.

STEPHEN FRY

Introduction

Thank you, ladies and gentlemen, and welcome to the Victoria Palace and *Hysteria!* I'm afraid you won't be quite so pleased when I tell you there is some rather unfortunate news. It's my job to have to break it to you: at the last minute the word 'fuck' had to pull out of the show. This is largely due to the presence of the cameras, so the word 'fuck' won't be making an appearance this evening. I know a lot of you will have come expecting to see the hilarious antics of the word 'fuck' and his family, 'fucker', 'fuck', 'fucks', 'fucking', 'fuck-buster', 'wild fuck under the table', but they will none of them, sadly, be here. However, it's not all bad news. Very kindly, at the last minute, we have some understudies who've agreed to step in. The word 'bother' will be playing the part of the word 'fuck' through the evening, and the word 'gosh' will be doubling as 'hellshit', 'bitch' and 'piss'. And very luckily, literally just this minute, the word 'blimey' agreed to take on the part of the word 'clitoris', which doesn't actually appear in the show anyway, but it's as well to be safe.

So, just before we begin, a word or two about the cause that has brought us all here this evening. You know, we talk a great deal, don't we, about safe . . . safe . . . well, safe sex, really. Of course, by that I don't mean making love to a strong box. (I just say that to lighten the tone.) There are hundreds of ways, aren't there, of enjoying safe carnal relations, sexual congress, love-making, coitus, copulation, coition – there are hundreds of words for it. Fucking is another one, of course. And I thought that to help us through this minefield it would be a good idea if here on stage – with the help, obviously, of one or two volunteers – I showed you some of the principles of safe sex. So let's welcome our volunteer couple, Dawn French and Hugh Laurie.

ROWAN ATKINSON, DAWN FRENCH,
STEPHEN FRY, HUGH LAURIE

Safe Sex Demonstration

SF: And you're going to demonstrate some safe and some unsafe positions for us, is that right?

HL: That's about the size of it, Stephen.

SF: Size isn't important, Hugh. I thought you knew that. Thank you. All right. Can you go straightaway, please, into unsafe position number 1?

Stephen Fry and volunteer couple

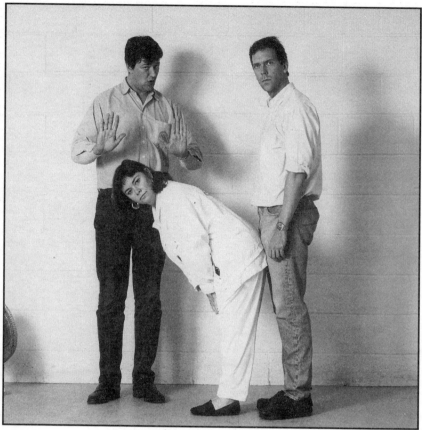

Unsafe position number 1

SF: Now that position, ladies and gentlemen, that position is unsafe. That is an unsafe position . . . and break.

Thank you, thank you very much. Relax.

Would you now like to show us, please, the safe version of that position? Thank you.

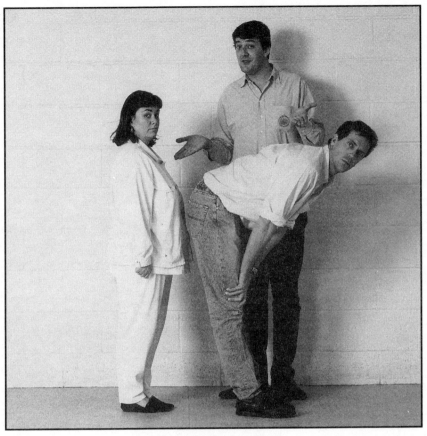

Safe position number 1

And this position is perfectly safe. And break. *And break.* Thank you. All right.

Can we have a look now, please – when you're ready, and in your own good time – at unsafe position number 2, unsafe position number 2?

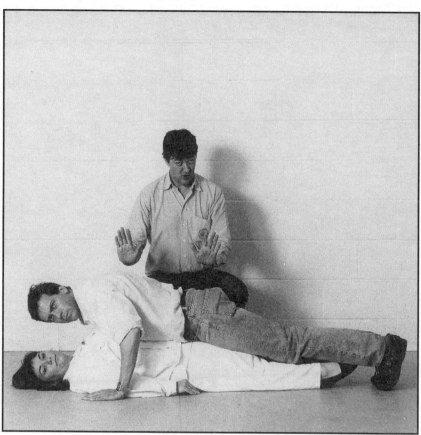

Unsafe position number 2

SF: This position is most awfully unsafe. And break. *And break.*
And if you could now show us, please, the safe version of this position?

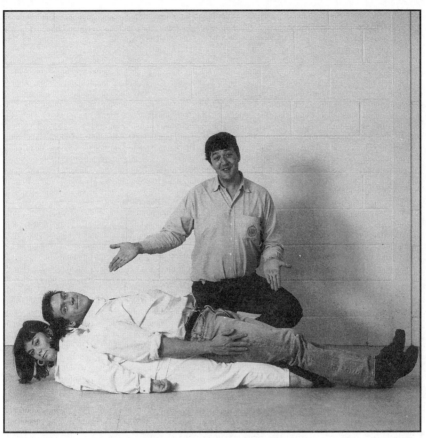

Safe position number 2

A position there that's perfectly safe. And relax.
Now please may we see unsafe position number 3, unsafe position
number 3?

Unsafe position number 3

SF: This position is radically unsafe.
May we now have a glimpse of the safe version of this position?

Safe position number 3

This position is perfectly safe. A perfectly safe position. Thank you. And now let's have a look at our most dangerous position, which is unsafe position number 4. This is a very, very unsafe position. If you'd like to assume it, please.

DF: Good luck!

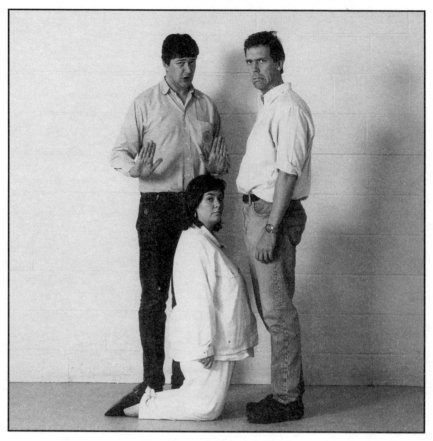

Unsafe position number 4

SF: This position is most awfully unsafe.

DF: I'm feeling unsafe. I'm feeling unsafe.

SF: Yes, I think you'd better break out of it as quickly as you can, please. And now to see the safe version of this position, we need a third demonstrator. So would you welcome, please, Mr Mel Smith. (*Rowan Atkinson walks on.*) I'm so sorry. I always get them muddled up.

HL: Hi, Mel.

SF: All right. And now can we quickly see, please, the safe version of that fourth dangerous position, the safe version?

Safe position number 4

There we are. And break. Well, I hope we've all picked up something there.

RA: I rather hope we haven't!

SF: Yes, I hope we haven't picked something up. You're quite right. Thank you to our three demonstrators. Many thanks.

STEVEN WRIGHT

I got food poisoning today. I don't know when I'm gonna use it.

I was walking down the street, there was a sign stapled to a telephone pole. It said, 'Reward. Lost $50. If found, just keep it.'

*E*very morning I get up and I make instant coffee and I drink it so I'll have enough energy to make the regular coffee.

*O*ne time, right in the middle of a job interview, I took out a book and I started reading. The guy said, 'What the hell are you doing?'

I said, 'Let me ask you this. If you were in a vehicle and you were travelling at the speed of light and then you turned your lights on, would they do anything?'

He said, 'I don't know.'

I said, 'Forget it, then. I don't want to work for you.'

*S*ponges grow in the ocean – that kills me. I wonder how much deeper the ocean would be if that didn't happen?

RUBY WAX

Ruby enters with a camera. She starts snapping the audience.

Could you all, like, club together and lick your lips? Would you just do that? Or lick anybody else's lips? Do something, OK, because you won't believe this. That's fabulous. No, I like to send photos of myself to my mother so she can show her friends. She says, 'This is my daughter with her public,' and then they show her pictures. They say, 'This is my daughter with her husband,' and my mother grows another pile to add to her collection. She blames me. She says I'm the reason she can't sit down. She blames me for the entire ruination of her body. This is a woman who attempted a tummy tuck in her eighth month of pregnancy, I swear to God. Well, anyway, who cares?

It's spring, and I'm about to get my licence back. I was banned for a year. You know, I didn't think you'd do that to me in this country. I didn't do anything wrong. I was a teeny weeny bit drunk. I just pulled over to some policemen, and I said, 'How the fuck do I get off this roundabout?' They pulled me out of the car. You know, I had to walk on that line. This is not a good time to show off my two years of ballet training. Anyway I had to be a pedestrian, which was awful because when I was a driver I used to use pedestrians as target practice. I hated it. I hated all that air out there, you know?

I just hate health in general, really. You know what I hate the most is those natural food shops – you know those? What does that mean, they sell turf? What is *organic*? Just another word for dirty fruit, for God's sake. You know, when they sell that tofu – girls, girls, have you ever had a yeast infection? You know what I'm saying? It's not two hundred miles away from what tofu looks like. And they sell you

those candy bars, you know, made out of that stuff pigs won't even eat – soya. And they wazz it up: they put the word 'ola' at the end of it – Yummola, you know, Crunchola, Retchola, they put it on. Then they've got those natural shoe shops. What does that mean? It comes with the doggie stuff already on it? You know, I spend hours of the week shaving off natural. I don't want to eat it for lunch or wear it on my foot, for God's sake.

In America we don't care about natural so much. We just care if we look young, you know – that's the thing. I mean, look at you in this country. You don't care what you look like. Look at you, you let yourself go. You have old people walking in the street. Old people unashamed in public. Disgusting. It's an old country. You don't care if they look old. And your most famous people are dead, so what do you care? I come from a young country. We have to look young. And we'll do anything for it. Suck the glands out of a monkey. Bathe in formaldehyde, that's one. But the biggie now is human placenta. That's afterbirth to you, creamers and moisturizers to us. The first sign of a crow's foot, they run to the maternity ward with a bucket. They don't come to see their baby: they come for the leftovers. 'Toss out that kid and cut the cord' – you know what I'm saying?

But the men here are starting to look like the men in America. That's caught on here. The men here used to look like dead halibut (no offence), and now they look like athletes. Everybody wants to look like an athlete. Just tell me why. Because, you know, when I was going to high school the biggest jerks in the place were the athletes. They used to get a degree in bringing your pencil. You used to use their head as a dartboard and they wouldn't know it, right? And now they're on television doing those commercials for jeans, telling me what jeans to wear with a translator standing by to interpret the grunts. Their pecs are, like, blown out beyond recognition, so the alligator on the Adidas shirt is now 40 feet long from their over-extended pecs. You know what it is – these men have breasts I've only dreamed about. There's no willy any more, that's been pulverized by the mondo-thighs. You know, so hard you can like rebound a speeding bullet off it.

Huge thighs, right, so there's no willy. So what's in its place? What's in its place? The Filofax. Yes. This is the leather-bound representative of what used to be in their pants. The bigger the better, so they sit up all night copying the phone book into it, so it's really big. 'Hey, I've got five inches of restaurants in Croydon. On your knees, woman!' It's true. I'm not making this up. Yesterday, I swear to God, I saw a Filofax carrying a human being. It's true, I swear to God.

Well, I don't know why you're smirking because this whole country is getting Americanized, totally Americanized. You know, when I got here twelve years ago I was ashamed. I was ashamed that people would hear my adenoids, and they would blame me for Vietnam and congratulate me on going to the moon. You can look in my passport: I've been in neither one of these places. And the most degrading thing is when the English waitresses try to be pert like us Americans. Pert and tight like they can hold their pencil between their buttocks. Looks like they're just naughty Doris Days. And they pull those lips back over their head so you're looking at wall-to-wall teeth. And then they bark, 'Y'all have a nice one,' in your face. Very flattering.

Well, let me just tell you, it seems fair to me. You gave us London Bridge; we gave you the 'Whopper'. Thank you very much. Thank you.

Whenever I fill in an application, it says, 'In case of emergency, notify...' I put 'Doctor'. What the hell is my mother going to do? STEVEN WRIGHT

28 ☆ ROWAN ATKINSON

ROWAN ATKINSON

Tom, Dick and Harry

Ladies and gentlemen, welcome to our church. Would it were a happier occasion, for we are gathered here today to pay our last respects to Thomas Fairclough, Richard Mason and Harold Walker – Tom, Dick and Harry as they were known to all of us. Three stout fellows of our village who will be sorely missed.

Tom, sadly, was blind, an affliction he bore with great fortitude, especially considering he was also deaf. His only power was that of speech and song, and we all recall his enormous voice joining lustily in our hymn-singing. Of course, being blind and deaf, Tom never actually knew what hymn we were singing, which seemed appropriate because we never knew what hymn he was singing either. In fact, if we had to be frank with each other, Tom didn't actually know any hymns. Thus it is with deep gratitude that we recall the day when Colonel Grant, using only a sense of touch through the medium of a clenched fist, actually broke through to Tom and got him to shut up.

Needing guidance through the darkness of life, Tom was lucky to have a friend like Dick. Dick had perfect eyesight and would gladly lead Tom wherever he wanted to go. Unfortunately, since Dick was also deaf, he couldn't actually hear where Tom wanted to go. Yet, like Tom, Dick never complained about his afflictions. Well, he couldn't. He was dumb. But, blessed with the gift of vision, though stone-deaf, he was a tremendous fan of Bananarama.

Being such an idiosyncratic pair, deaf to the world about them, Tom and Dick were lucky to have the permanent companionship of Harry. Harry could literally hear a pin drop, although, being blind and dumb, he could not see to pick it up or ask anyone else to stand on it.

And so, as individuals, they were sadly afflicted. But together they were in possession of all of God's senses, weren't they? And it is together that we remember them. Together at their job, checking eggs at the battery farm – Dick would look for the cracks, Tom would complain to the foreman, and Harry would do the listening to Radio 1. Likewise in the evening, when they had returned from work, they would all sit on the big couch in front of the television – Dick watching it, Harry listening to it, and Tom remarking that rubbish like this just wasn't worth the licence fee.

Sadly, as we all know, three days ago their peaceful lives were ended. Dick saw the combine harvester, Harry heard the combine harvester, but neither could cry out. Tom, who could have cried out, never had the faintest idea what hit him. And so they were all harvested together, blended into oneness at last and now, we trust, are in heaven, as happy as any in that immortal host, for Dick will see the angels' choir, Harry will hear the angels' choir and, no doubt, Tom will ruin it for everybody.

I bought this little thing for my car. If you put it on your car, it sends this noise so that when you drive through the woods deer won't run in front of your car. I installed it backwards by accident. I was driving down the street with a herd of deer chasing me. STEVEN WRIGHT

VIC REEVES

'I Remember Punk Rock'

Good evening, ladies and gentlemen. Yes, I am Britain's top light entertainer, Mr Vic Reeves, and I'd like to ask a simple question of any of you people out there – you and you and you, of course: does anybody remember punk rock?

A simple few. But for those few I'd like to sing a song tonight, ladies and gentlemen, entitled 'I Remember Punk Rock' because I do, and I'd like to sing it for you. If the orchestra are ready?

> You know I remember punk rock
> Like it was only yesterday.
> Oh, Mr Buzzcock on my shoulders singing
> In that extra special way.

> You know, I remember punk rock,
> And I recall those melodies
> By the Clash, the Adverts, Wire, Eater,
> Not to mention ATV.

> Well, Generation X sang so sweetly,
> Whilst the Pistols ate their lunch.
> The Damned have tea with the Lurkers
> While Sex Respects enjoy brunch.

> You know, I remember punk rock,
> And I recall those melodies
> By the Clash, the Adverts, Wire, Eater,
> Not to mention ATV.

Oh, well, the Vibrators sang so tenderly,
While 999 had brunch.
Richard Hell had the Slits round for coffee,
And Slobber and Dodger have too.

You see, I remember punk rock
Like it was only yesterday.
Oh, Mr Buzzcock on my shoulders singing
In that extra special way.

Thank you very much, ladies and gentlemen.

*M*y mother used to feed me pancakes when I was little. Instead of maple syrup she switched to truth serum. I'd be eating the pancakes, saying, 'I'm the one who broke the window.'

But I caught on to this. I realized that every time I ate pancakes, a few hours later I got the hell beat out of me.

Then one day she said, 'Steven, you want some pancakes?'

I said, 'No, I don't like pancakes.'

She said, 'How about some waffles?'

I said, 'Yeah, I'll have some waffles.'

A few hours later I got the hell beat out of me.

STEVEN WRIGHT

Gay

SF: D'you know what I'd like to know?

HL: Have you told me before?

SF: No.

HL: Well, then, how could I possibly?

SF: I'd like to know why, oh why, oh why, the word 'gay' has been so ruthlessly hijacked from our beloved English language.

HL: I agree with your question one hundred per cent. 'Gay' used to be such a lovely word.

SF: A lovely word. I used to use it all the time.

HL: Oh, yes. Can't any more.

SF: No, no. Can't any more. It's been taken away from us.

HL: That's right. No longer can ordinary people, such as we, use an ordinary word like 'gay' in an ordinary example of the great British sentence.

SF: Without people thinking that you mean 'poofy'.

HL: It's a disgrace, a damned shame.

SF: And there's another one: 'poofy'. You can't say that any more.

HL: Of course you can't.

SF: Used to.

HL: All the time.

SF: So did I. Now, of course, nowadays, people just think you mean 'arse bandit'.

HL: Well, you see, there you go again, now you come to think of it – 'arse bandit'. Perfectly decent couple of words. Used to use them all the time.

SF: So did I.

HL: 'Would you care to have a go on the arse bandit?' one used to ask, quite innocently.

SF: Yes. 'Back in a minute, darling. I'm just picking up the arse bandit from the menders.'

HL: Yes, yes, for example. Now, of course . . .

SF: Nowadays . . .

HL: Well, people think you mean 'homosexual'.

SF: That's right. And there's another one. When did you last use the word 'homosexual' in its proper context?

HL: Exactly. It's such a lovely word.

SF: Oh, it's one of the great words.

HL: Yes. 'My word, Mary,' I used to say to my wife, 'the garden's looking very homosexual this morning.'

SF: 'Landlord, I'll have two foaming pints of your most homosexual beer, please.'

HL: 'Oh, and a packet of arse bandits as well.'

SF: 'And keep the change.'

HL: Now, of course . . .

SF: Nowadays . . .

HL: Well, they'd just laugh at you, wouldn't they?

SF: That's right. Oh, well, I'm going down to the dry cleaner's to pick up a couple of screaming benders. Are you coming?

HL: That seems like a good idea. We could take them home and go to bed with them.

I was driving down the highway, saw a sign that said 'Next Rest Area 25 Miles'. I said, 'Wow, that's pretty big. People must get really tired around here.'
STEVEN WRIGHT

HARRY ENFIELD, CRAIG FERGUSON AND JERRY HALL

Jerry's Lucky Night

HE: You can't beat a good pub, can you? Oh, no. You can't beat a really good pub.

CF: That's certainly true.

HE: If you want a bloody awful night out, you can't beat a really good pub.

CF: What are you on about, eh? If you hate pubs so much, how come you're in here every night?

HE: I come in here to meet people, don't I?

CF: Well, go on then.

HE: What?

CF: Meet someone.

HE: I already have.

CF: Who?

HE: You. I meet you here every night.

CF: Why don't you just admit it?

HE: What?

CF: You come here to meet women. You just don't have the guts. That's the difference between us, you see. I've got the guts. I just can't be bothered. I'm cool. You're just plain pathetic.

HE: Oh, yeah?

CF: Yeah.

HE: All right, then. Watch this.

CF: What's this?

HE: You'll see. (*Writes on cigarette packet.*) There you go.

CF: (*Reads*) Nobby. By the Gent's. Dog and Duck.

HE: That's me, right? Now, watch this. (*Walks to door and chucks cigarette packet outside.*) How about that, eh?

CF: Oh, very nice. Yeah. You threw a packet of cigarettes out the door.

HE: Exactly. Now all I've got to do is wait.

CF: For what?

HE: For the sexy ladies to walk down the street, see the fags, pick them up, read the writing and bring them in here to me. That's the way to meet women. Make them come to you. I'm smooth, you see. That's the difference between us.

CF: You're bloody barking mad, that's the difference between us. What woman in her right mind's going to pick your cigarettes off the street?

HE: Princess Di? Fatima Whitbread? Jerry Hall?

CF: Ha! Jerry Hall? What the hell is Jerry Hall going to be doing in Peckham?

HE: Same as me. Looking for action. I don't know. Nothing on telly, Mick's on tour, hops on the bus to Peckham, doesn't she? Walking past the pub, goes down to tie up her shoelaces, clocks the fags, *wallop*, it's Jerry's lucky night.

CF: All right, Mr Smoothie, let's say Jerry walks in here, hands you the fags. What are you going to say to her?

HE: Something smooth like, 'Hello, darling. What's a lovely bird like you doing with a name like Jeremy? Here, get your laughing gear round that.' (*Proffers beer glass to imaginary Jerry.*)

CF: She's from Texas, you prat. They don't have laughing gear in Texas.

HE: Well, Mick has, hasn't he?

CF: Mick has, yes. He could get his laughing gear round Texas in fact, couldn't he? Nobby, do me a favour, please.

HE: What?

CF: When a woman walks in, leave the talking to me. I know how to talk to women. I understand them. I know what they're after.

HE: Oh, yeah. What's that, then?

CF: Mystery. A man of mystery, that's what turns them on. Jerry Hall walks in here. I lay you odds she looks at me. I don't say a thing. I let my face do the talking. And my hand as well sometimes. See, what does that remind you of? (*Adopts Clint Eastwood pose.*)

HE: A whale on acid.

CF: We'll see who she prefers.

HE: You're too right, mate. I'm ready.

CF: So am I. I'm hot – hot but cool.

HE: I've got my motor running, don't you worry, pal. (*Pause.*) Don't look like she's coming, does it?

CF: No. No. Shame, that.

HE: Shall we go for a curry, then?

CF: Why not? Can't hang about, too busy. But, let's face it, if she had come in, she'd have gone for the mystery man.

HE: No, mate, the smoothie.

CF: Mystery man.

HE: Smoothie.

CF: Mystery man.

HE: Smoothie.

CF: Mystery man, mystery man, mystery man . . .

(*While this is gong on Jerry Hall enters, carrying a cigarette packet. Harry and Craig clock her and are so terrified and overcome with desire that they clutch each other like little children.*)

JH: Excuse me, gentlemen. Is one of y'all Nobby?

(*Too scared to speak, they shake their heads.*)

JH: Shoot! I thought it was my lucky night. Bye now!

(*Jerry turns and exits. Pause.*)

CF: I didn't fancy her anyway.

HE: Me neither.

MORWENNA BANKS

Diseasure

Yes, I do know how you get a diseasure. First of all you do go into the swimming pool and get a mushroom on your foot wot is called a Veronica. And this is like a tiny snake maked out of flea sick. And it does wriggle all the way up your leg, and it does eat your sausage meat febus it is very hungry and there wasn't any plankson in the swimming pool.

Then when it gets to your belly button it does try and get out, but luckily your button has been sewed up with cat gut so it can never come undone, except in Heaven, if Jesus wanted to have a look at your dinner and see how many lungs you got.

So then the Veronica haves to try and crawl out your lug holes. Then you must go to the doctor, and he does light a match and have a look in your brain and he says, 'How many fingers have I got?' And if you can only count one finger, then you are mental, and you must live in an ambliance and have your arms sewed together, and wear pants on your head, and only eat bigjobs. And you must say this thing, 'Tarzan in the jungle / Having a bit of fun / Trying to stick a monkey / Up a Rangatang's bum.' Yes, you must.

And you must have all your hair cut off, and sewing on your head, febus they have taken out your brain with the electric tweezers so that you do not get rabies or punch an old lady on the bosoms. And if you are very poorly, then the old nun with the tea towel and the big teeth might give you nedecin and make you better, but she might be too busy putting fly spray on the poor black babies. So you might have to sick up the Veronica into a bucket of disinfenton or eat twelve Mars Bars, plus one plus two, and wait for the Veronica to pop up and say,

'More tea, please, Vicar,' and then you grab it by the neck and pull. And all your body does go inside out, and you do look like a butcher shop. And that is wot is a diseasure. It is. It's TRUE.

EDDIE IZZARD

Ah, good evening, welcome. Just before I go into the stuff, I've been reading a very good book. You must read this book. It's called *Sex, Drugs and Me* by J. R. Hartley. It's a real cracker. It's the sequel to *Fly Fishing*, right? He's taken all the same characters but just taken it a stage further, and it's great, it really is . . . I was just reading it all night, you know? And I couldn't get to sleep all night . . . so scary . . . and wonderful. And then the next day I went out and bought all the gear and . . . um . . . it's great.

Also I've been reading another book . . . the Bible. Not the J. R. Hartley version, not that version, the extended one. That was really good stuff.

Er, Easter, essentially . . . quite a heavy time for Jesus . . . um . . . 'cos he died . . . crucified . . . and at the end, at the crucifixion, talking to the disciples on the cross, saying, 'My disciples. My disciples, I must leave you now. Will you – will you, be true to me?'

'Yes, we will, Lord. We've had a chat, and, er, it's on our To Do list. Yes:

1. Be true to the Lord
2. Loaf of bread
3. Pint of milk.

Yes, gonna do that.'

'And have you decided how you will remember this day for now and for ever more?'

'Yes! We've decided chocolate eggs. That seems favourite, Lord. And we're gonna get a bunny rabbit in there somewhere as well, with big ears, 'cos the kids love it, you know? It's great. We're gonna have hollow chocolate eggs, ones that you can open up, and they've got scrummy things inside, you know, like Smarties and small Mars Bars. Not the big ones. Small ones, 'cos the big ones won't fit, you see. Call them 'funsize', Lord, because they are fun to eat. You eat them . . . ooh, it's fun, you see. And . . . ah . . . and all the eggs are covered with crinkly papers. You can crinkle them up really small and go ping!

(*Demonstrates. Pretends to be hit. Wags finger.*)

'Oh, no. Don't do that . . . Take that, Judas!'

'And, Lord, with the egg, what we're gonna do, you're gonna have a mug as well! Sounds great. And we can have something written on the mug, something like "The Lord is my Shepherd. I shall not want . . . more chocolate until next year . . . because I feel sick." '

Because it is a bit strange, isn't it? Small children must come to their parents and say, 'What's the chocolate egg about?'

'Ah . . . Jesus was crucified and . . . er . . . it's very painful . . . and . . . er . . . Piss off, will you?'

'What about the bunny rabbit? What's the bunny rabbit with the big ears that comes and gives out the eggs?'

'Ah. Jesus was crucified . . . and . . . er . . . on the left they crucified Barabbas, Barabbas the thief . . . ah, yes . . . and on the right-hand side they crucified a . . . a bunny rabbit. And that was the beginning of animal experiments, you see. Very bad days. Lipstick . . . and it went wrong . . . and . . . er . . . Piss off, will you?'

Easter. Bad time for Jesus. Other bad times recently, bad times . . . The only real good thing, the thing that gets you up in the morning and you think, 'Ooh, things are still good!' is the fact that Mrs Thatcher is having an extraordinarily bad time. You get up in the morning and you go, 'Oh, she's having a bad time – brilliant!' (*Sings and dances with joy.*)

You know, you can look like sick in the morning when you look in the mirror, but still it's great and you go, 'Hey!', you know? Because for eleven years, eleven years, people lost their jobs, and they said, 'I've lost my job. I'm sixty years old. My life is shattered!' And she, particularly her, she said, 'Go! Get another job! On the bicycle thing, drive off, retrain at sixty – go on!'

And now she's lost her job, and she's saying, 'My life is shattered!' I think we're all saying, 'Er, Job Club! Go on Thatcher, get down there! Get some stamps and two phone calls.'

She's phoning the United Nations. 'Can I have a job?'

'No! No! We hate you.'

And also she said to women, she said, 'All women, get back in your houses,' and she's back in her house now, and she's saying, 'Ooh, this is crap!' True! And for eleven years, she'd see things and she'd immediately get on the phone and say, 'Do this!'

And they'd say, 'Oh, all right, then.'

And now she sees things on the television and she's going, 'Do this!' and they're going, 'No, Thatcher! And you've got big hair as well!'

She did, didn't she? Remember 1979 came in, she had hair, we go, 'OK.' In 1985 it was bigger. We were going, 'Oh.' When she resigned it was up *here*! And I think the idea was: 'If I can't get a crown on, I'll have bloody big hair!'

Also I'm happy at the moment because I've just finished my autobiography. I'm very pleased. It's called *Eddie Izzard: The Wilderness Years*. And we're gonna sell it in all the good bookshops. And just for the crack we're gonna sell it in the bad bookshops as well. Well, give 'em a break. You know, shops that have got one book . . . and an egg . . . and an elephant. 'Yeah, we're a bad bookshop. I'm sorry . . .'

I'll say, 'You can sell that.'

'Oh, thank you very much. Thanks.'

I had a rough childhood. You probably all know I had to escape from Nazi Germany in 1937. Well, we were living in Munich. My father was the Liberal Party candidate for Bavaria . . . in the '33 elections, you know. He was standing on jobs, pensions, freedom of speech – good liberal values – and he was up against Hermann Goering, who was on 'Vote for me or I'll kill you'. Good Nazi values. And we were losing hands down, and we had to escape. So under the cover of darkness my mother went down to the river, and on the river bank she took some reeds, and she took some mud, and she fashioned them into the shape of a U-boat. And it floated off down the river, and I escaped. It was great.

And I was brought up after that by . . . wolves! They were out yachting one day and . . . It was great. It was wonderful. You know, it was great being brought up by wolves as a kid. It was wonderful. They gave me a name. They called me 'Rrrr'. And they taught me all the stuff – hunting, fishing, backgammon, all that. And wolves are natural at fishing. They wait by fast-flowing rivers, and then when a big fish comes along, just at the right moment, they reel it in really, really good. Land it, you know? Cook it gas mark 4 with some herbs. And we were wolves – we were young, we were crazy. We'd make love in the moonlight . . . They would, *they* would . . . I'd watch and say, 'No, no, I'm full, thank you.' And we were hunting all the time. (*He sings:*)

We're hunting,
We're hunting those things,
Those things over there.
We're wolves,
We're hunting them,
We're not sure what they are . . .

It was a crap song, but we didn't care. There was no choir practice, and we just went with it, you know? There were nineteen wolves and me, and I was trying to blend in, going, 'Woof, woof.'

And these bears would stand there and say, 'Ooh, what's that?'

I'd go, 'Hi. I'm a wolf. Catch you later!' (*Mimes running.*) And we'd be chasing these things – they'd turn out to be antelopes – so it was great because we ate them, and after about twenty minutes they put on a real lead, so we had a discussion and agreed to move our legs as well. That really helped.

One of the key things if you are hunting, you've got to move towards them, otherwise they go away. And, whooah, could those wolves move! 'Cos they'd got four legs between them. Four legs each, not four legs between them. Because that would be one leg every five wolves, wouldn't it? If you had that, you'd have one wolf on one leg, hopping, dragging four wolves behind him on three legs. And that hunting method isn't quite as efficient as your basic wolvine running-after-them kind. So, *whoosh!* Off they went, and I couldn't keep up with them. Two legs, you know? So I took to driving a small red car. It was great. It was a hatchback. It was roomy, so I said, 'Guys, get in the back!' And I turned the blow heater up full so it blew their ears back.

And we were thundering down the bayou there, and the antelope were getting really frightened. They'd go, 'Oh, my God! They're catching up!', 'cos all the wolves were on spacehoppers, right?

And we were behind them in the car going *vroom, vroom,* and I wound down the window and said, 'Get the gun! Shoot! Shoot!'

They said, 'We're wolves. We haven't got guns.'

I said, 'Oh, no!' We couldn't do anything. We'd just drive along, and the antelope were grinning. So I just leaned out of the window and went, 'Rrrr! That's my name!'

It was funny in those days anyway. That's all from me.

FASCINATING AIDA WITH MARIE HELVIN

'Lieder'

Doesn't matter if you sing out of tune
So long as you're German;
Doesn't matter if you can hardly croon
So long as you're German;
So if you haven't got a note in your head
Put on a silly accent instead,
And people will stop wishing you were dead,
So long as you're German.

Doesn't matter if the notes are all wrong
And people are squirmin'.
Just make the tune up as you go along –
Pretend you're German.
And if your voice sounds like it's coming through a strainer,
Sing it out of synch, like Marlene;
And soon you'll be compared to Lotte Lenya,
Who was German.

Nicht hinauslehnen sprecht Gesang
Zauberflöte Wunderbar
Johnny,
Wiener Schnitzel, Boris Becker, Sturm und Drang, Cooch Behar,
Johnny . . .

So if you've ever wondered what you have to do
To sound like a Hun,
Just chain smoke from the tender age of two:
That's how it's done.

And when the audiences are all walking out,
Just make believe that you're a Kraut.
Then open your mouth and shout
In German
In German
In German
In German

Auf Deutsch! Jawohl!

FRENCH AND SAUNDERS

School Sketch

Dawn French stands at a lectern. Jennifer Saunders sits by her side gazing into the audience.

DF: Well done, 4C, for that lovely disco dancing to the tune of 'When Will I be Famous?' by the band . . . Brothers, which was very suitable for my theme for assembly this week, which is 'achievement'. I don't know how many of you saw the lovely David Attenborough documentary on television last night, but in it there was another item that illustrates my sub-theme for assembly this week, which is 'If at first you don't succeed, try, try again'.

JS: (*Stands up and points into audience.*) Right, you. Yes, you, Mary Gordon. You know who you are. See me after.

DF: In the documentary, girls, there was a tiny butterfly inside a cocoon. In order to escape from the cocoon to freedom, the butterfly had to nibble a little hole and push its head through. After much perseverance and struggle, the butterfly did indeed push its head through to freedom, and the moral of this story is, girls, if your holes are too small, just keep on pushing . . .

JS: (*Stands up; DF sits down.*) What? You, yes, *you*, ugly girl there, 2C. Don't look at your friends. I'm talking to you. Stand up. Right. I'm glad you've stood up. Can you see something about that girl, Miss Barnes? Yes. She is wearing tan tights. There is a rule in this school. Nobody below the fifth form is allowed to wear tan tights. And there is a reason for that rule.

DF: Except for staff, isn't it?

JS: Except for staff, Miss Barnes. I will not have . . .

DF: Staff are allowed . . .

JS: Staff are allowed to wear tan tights. I will not have . . .

DF: But not track suits.

JS: Not track suits. I will not have . . .

DF: Except the PE Department.

JS: The PE Department are allowed to wear track suits. Right. Sit down. I'll see you afterwards. Is there anything else before I go on? I have in my hand here a detention list, and it appears to me that this list gets longer every day. These girls will stay behind after school: Fiona Cotter Craig (jewellery); Pauline Wilde (pregnant again – Pauline, are you?); Jo Laurie, Alice Fay, Felicity O'Brien (sitting on radiators). I will not have that selfish sort of behaviour from girls in this school. We do not spend nearly £100 a year on school heating to warm your nasty little bottoms, do we?

DF: No, we don't.

JS: I do not come round your houses and sit on your radiators, do I?

DF: Yes, you do.

JS: No, I told you, Miss Barnes. Is there anything else before we go? No, you. Yes, you at the back, grey perm, Geography, Mrs Griffiths, is it? Shut up, woman.

DF: I just wanted to talk about . . .

JS: Now, you shut up as well now, Miss Barnes. Hands on head. There has been a lowering of standards in this school. An increase in shameful and shoddy behaviour. Just the other night, while I was cruising around town on my way home from school, not only did I see three Manor School girls not wearing regulation berets – you know who you are – but as I was passing the bus terminus I saw four girls entwined around male creatures.

DF: I was one of those, Head . . .

JS: I will not have that evil, sordid, carnal, lascivious sort of behaviour. It belongs in the sewer. I do not know what goes on in the horrible, stench-filled little hovels that you all call home, but I will not have it while you're in school uniform. If you think I am being unfair, if you think I am wrong, then you can come and see me in my office. We can have a friendly chat about it. All right. I am an approachable person. That is my job. Who laughed?

DF: Not me, not . . .

JS: Right, I will see every girl in this school in my office after assembly. I want to see you down on your knees, begging me for forgiveness. I'm going to whip down your panties and spank some sense into those . . .

DF: Head, Head, can I volunteer for that punishment, please?

JS: Not again, Miss Barnes. Right, any girls interested in cricket. Well, see me on the playing fields after school. Thank you. Carry on, Miss Barnes.

DF: School, fall out.

HARRY ENFIELD

Stavros

Good evening, ladies and gents. My name is Stavros. I'm afraid tonight I don't have my moustache because how come it get cut back by the Tory government, innit. Oops, little bit of politic there. My name Elton Ben Goodbye Yellow Brick Road, innit.

My name's Stavros, and, as you may know, I've got a little kebab shop down in Bethnal Green, East London. It's only a little one, but as the ladies they keep telling me, it's not the size that count, it's what you do with it, innit? No, it's only little, but, you know, there's not too much competition. Just one Kentuckity Fried Chick, but nobody really like to go in there. I don't know why. Maybe it's because the food tastes like a load of dumpy dogshit or what. Now we're always very busy though, especially at 11 o'clock when the pubs they shut. 'Time, genitals, please,' and we get the bloody Charge of the Light Ale Brigade come down. I'm a tell you, some of them are real pesky little pissers or what. This bloke come in the other day, right. He's pissed out of his head, right. He goes, 'Stavros, you greasy bast.'

I said to him, 'I'm no grease. I'm always very clean and tide, you cheeky little cock-sucking monkey sod.'

He said to me, 'Well, if you so clean, how come every time I'm a have a kebab from here I'm a puke up after?'

I'm a say, 'Maybe it's got something to do with the thirteen pints of lager you have beforehand.'

He say, 'Well, anyway, you donna speak props.'

I say, 'After fifteen pints of lager, mate, you don't speak so bloody good yourself. Bloody terrible, bloody monkey sod.'

I get a lot of nutters come in my shop, though, right? This bloke the other day, he come in. I say, 'You wanna kebab?'

Stavros *with* moustache

He say, 'No. I'm come to canvas.'

I say, 'I don't need canvas. I've got very nice lino, thank you very much.'

He say, 'No. It's for the General Erection.' He say, 'Please vote Conservative. Please, please, please will you vote Conservative? Please?'

I'm a say to him, 'You can ask me to vote Conservative until the cows they come home, but I'm not a bloody going to. And get your head away from my knob.'

I donna really like this government myself because, the way I look at it, there's some peeps that are very good out of it. They get tax cuts, and they get shares in British-bloody-never-bloody-work-Telefuckingcom or what. Round Hackney, right, where I live, in bloody Hackney, you go to use a phone box, right, they never bloody work. The only peeps who use phone box, the only thing they use it for is to have a crap, innit. Terrible thing, it really is. But on the one hand you got these peeps; on the other hand, though, a lot of peeps, they haven't not got bollocks, innit. Women, for instance, they've got none. That's it. No. It's changed, though, because when I first come in England and my wife thirty years ago – She's good, my wife, you know her? She's not here tonight but, you know, she's the spitting image of Penelope Keith except for the fact she's a little dumpy and Greek. But, other than that, she's just like her. Anyway, when we first come in England, right, it was the nineteen-fifths, right? It was the time when 'You don't never have it so bloody good,' say Mr Harold 'He Sent Him Back to Russia and Certain Death' Macmillan.

Oh, yes. So then, right, there was London job, but today that is no job, right, except in Hackney the only peeps who've got job are Puppies. You know these Puppies? Poncy, upwardly mobile peeps. I'm a donna like them. They come in the shop, right? I say, 'You wanna kebab?'

They say, 'Ugh, meat. No, we don't like meat. You got any coldsore?'

I say, 'Yeah. How many porsh you want?'

They say, 'No, I've already gotta Porsche and a Golf GTI.'

I say, 'Well, how come you got so much money, then? What you do for a job?'

They say, 'I'm a merchant banker.'

It's funny. I don't know how they know this Cockney rhyming slang!

And then, when they come to pay, right, they go, 'Hello, do you know me? American Excess?'

I say, 'No. I donna bloody know you, and I donna take no Barclay-bloody-four-eyed-bloody-bast-Alan-Whicker card. I can't even take a luncheon voucher any more since I get all the citizens coming in wanting naughty sexy spank Harvey Procter.'

Bloody terrible.

Thank you very much. Goodnight.

HELEN LEDERER

It's great to be here. It really is very, very funny. It's a real privilege, actually, to be asked to come and perform free – especially so. Thanks. Lovely. In fact, I think I'm the only one. The rest are being paid, so I feel great. Thank you very much for making me feel so special.

Anyway, I haven't actually been very well recently, in case any of you were worried. I thought you might be. I thought I had ME, you know, the yuppie flu, so I went to the doctor, and I said, 'I think I've got yuppie flu,' you see.

So he said, 'How much do you earn?' So I told him and he said, 'Yes, you're just run down.'

I wasn't going to be fobbed off. I asked for some tests, but, being the NHS, they couldn't offer me an immediate appointment date, obviously, so what he offered to do was place my notes in a time capsule and conceal them under the surgery floorboards, which I thought was quite encouraging.

Anyway, well, I know what I've got, actually. I've got hormonal imbalance. It's quite a neat label. It's not a problem if you've got hormonal imbalance: it just means that you don't lay eggs, well, not to EC standards anyway, in case anyone wondered. People might need to know that. I don't know. It's peculiar to me, possibly. So what they do, you see, to address it, is they have to give you more hormones. I don't know where they get them from. I don't like to pry, actually. They said it was from some laboratory in Switzerland. I think it was more like some sheep's bottom in the Lake District. That's what it smelt like.

The thing is, I know what the problem is. The real problem is I've just had a fling. I know, I was shocked. You see, what happened was

the phone went in the house, and I answered it because I wasn't doing anything else, obviously, and this voice said, 'Hello! How would you like to come for a dirty weekend in Paris?' And then there was silence and the voice said, 'I'm sorry. Have I shocked you?'

And I said, 'God, no. I was just packing.'

It was great. It was really romantic. When I say romantic, actually, I found it quite difficult to get aroused, really I did, because some things are just passion killers. I mean, a man naked except for a pair of socks is completely repellent to me, and then it's worse when they take them off because then you get that elastic pattern round the ankles, quite ugly. No, it cuts both ways. I remember he commented on the size of my Caesarian scar, and then I had to say, 'No, it isn't one. It's just that this slip's too tight.' But he was a very considerate lover, to be fair. He insisted on lying on the damp patch afterwards. He was a real Sir Walter Raleigh.

Anyway, so I got back from Paris and I thought to myself, am I actually in a long-term relationship? You know, I was panicking, and I thought, I am. So I immediately got my Filofax and set aside six months for the inevitable post-break-up grief, December through till June, because you can get some away-breaks in June which I thought I might be needing. No, but I mean there were problems. He was obsessed with my age. He was always asking me how old I was, and in the end I told him, 'OK. I'm thirty ... something, thirty-something.' You know, like the soap opera. I haven't actually seen the soap opera, but I have seen the Gold Blend coffee ad, which I think is quite a good role model to use. Anyway he was obsessed, and when you're thirty-plus, you're just too old for balloons, aren't you? Well, unless they come in packets of three, I always say – bit of a joke there.

It was a very, very mature relationship. We insisted on giving each other lots of space. In fact, we might have overdone it. I phoned him up the other day, and I said, 'What have you been doing since our last date?'

And he said, 'Well, got married, had a couple of kids, you know.' But I'm comfortable with that because ... I *am*. Why shouldn't he have other female friends? I know I do.

Anyway, on that happy note, have a lovely evening. Thanks very much. Goodnight.

ADRIAN EDMONDSON

Adrian Edmondson's Dirty Joke

My name's Adrian Edmondson. I don't know whether you remember me. I used to be very funny. But it's been a long time since *The Young Ones*, and I've just come to this benefit to boost my sadly flagging career, though I don't know what the fuck this do is all about. But I have got one joke left that I'd like to share with you all. Well, I've got two jokes, actually. I've got a little hole in my trousers, but it's not very funny. The second one, I hope, is slightly funnier.

There are two women sitting in the lounge of their house, and one of them says to the other (she's looking out of the window), she says, 'Oh, bugger me, there comes my husband with a big bunch of flowers. Oh, God, what am I going to do?'

And the other one says, 'What's the problem? It's a big bunch of flowers. It's very romantic, isn't it?'

She says, 'Romantic? This means I'm going to have to lie on my back all night with my legs wide open.'

And the other one says, 'Why? Haven't you got a vase?'

STEPHEN FRY

Again

Thank you, certainly, indeed, thank you, certainly, indeed, thank you, certainly, certainly, thank you indeed. A very warm welcome to the Sadlers Wells Theatre. It would be no exaggeration for me to say that I and the entire *Hysteria 2!* corporate structure are really quite pleased to see you here this evening. Thank you for coming. A word or two about the cameras that you see around you. They are shooting the entire performance, and certain highlights of it will be shown, certain highlights which may include you, of course, though they're slightly less likely to include *you. (He points to a member of the audience.)* No, I'm just being senselessly lovely there.

Before we begin I also want to warn those of you who are offended by bad language that there will be certain scenes which do contain some examples of shockingly loose and free grammar. There are malapropisms, misnomers and some complete misusages of words. Now, as far as I'm concerned, that's just the sign of a poor vocabulary, but there are those who insist on using it. Later on we'll have a tautology or two, a split infinitive and in one case somebody ending a sentence with a preposition. So to those of you who've led rather sheltered lives I ought to explain that ... Well, I can give you an example. In the second act someone uses the phrase 'Why don't you piss-heads fuck off?' Now, 'off', you see, is a preposition, and it's the kind of word that you should never end a sentence *with*. In fact. Actually.

The other thing I ought to come clean about is myself. I know this sounds a bit formal, but then I like formality. Wasn't it Oscar Wilde who was in prison for sodomy? I don't know why I said that. I've never made any secret of the fact that, sexually speaking, I don't.

I don't. I won't. I haven't, in fact, for about seven years. To be frank, the prospect of those damp, tufted areas of the human body holds no appeal for me whatsoever. The prospect of grinding and plunging and licking and frotting those moist mucous membranes leaves me appallingly cold. However, and it's a very large however, one of the largest ever recorded in this postal district, I do reserve the right to choose the gender of those people I don't go to bed with. I won't go to bed with anybody. I won't go to bed with girls or boys, men or women, ocelots, outboard motors, strimmers, architects . . . Anybody or anything that is willing, I'll not go to bed with. Now AIDS shouldn't change that. This appalling disease, whose miseries we are all here in our own small way to help try and alleviate, shouldn't change any of that. Safety, yes, prudence, certainly, but puritanism and intolerance, no go, because it is a fact that even if this awful virus were to increase a thousandfold in the next ten years, it would never, and could never, destroy as many lives as intolerance daily does.

TONY SLATTERY WITH RUBY WAX

Award Acceptance Speech

Ruby Wax walks onstage with gold envelope and an Oscar.

RUBY: And the nominations are: Stephanie Powers and all those guys who brought you that load of bull in *Matador*; Lady Diana Spencer for reviving *Manhood* in the Prince of Wales; and Tony Slattery for his performance as Fred Dineage in *How?: The Desperate Years*. And the winner is – TONY SLATTERY!

Tony enters, accepts award. Walks to microphone.

TONY: Your Royal Highness, my lords, ladies and gentlemen . . . Platitude platitude cliché banter platitude cliché. Cliché cliché weak quip coy self-deprecation mutter mutter mutter.

Well-rehearsed demeanour of complete bewilderment and vulnerability followed by carefully timed st-st-stutter to indicate sincerity and debilitating emotion.

Serious facial expression suddenly. Namedrop namedrop namedrop cliché hugely unconvincing rubbish about sharing the award.

Cliché cliché cliché rhetorical question about subsidized theatre pretend to get angry wait for Pavlovian applause largely from people who couldn't give a toss.

Shout shout shout declaim declaim declaim end of serious bit.

Lighten up a bit now. Anecdote anecdote anecdote in-joke in-joke gossip gossip gossip throwaway comment about the RSC, revealing hidden reserves of professional bitterness and envy.

Recognize casting director in audience. Focus focus focus beam beam beam ghastly ingratiating gesture.

End in sight now embark on stupefyingly complex and profoundly dull metaphor about encouraging new talent meander meander meander losing it losing it rambling quite badly sweat sweat sweat shouldn't have done a gram and a half.

Rush rush rush stumble panic stumble get to final pathetic joke and cock up the punchbag . . . the punch*line*!

A couple of beats, then blackout.

I'm a peripheral visionary. I can see into the future but just way off to the side.

I got a new dog. He's a paranoid retriever. He brings back everything because he's not sure what I threw him.

Went up to a tourist information booth. I walked up and I said, 'Yeah, so tell me about some people who were here last year.'
STEVEN WRIGHT

'Arise, Sir Jase!'

Rest in peace, great Olivier,
Hanged with the laurels of renown.
Let tears cease, great Olivier,
A nobler brow shall bear thy burnished crown.
Fame's on lease, great Olivier,
Glory just a torch that's handed down.
Who will fight your fights? Who will fill your tights?
I've an inkling who'll be twinkling
Now they've dimmed your lights.

It's going to be Jason Donovan.
It's going to be Lord Jason, wait and see.
He's taller and, ay, marry,
Something prettier than Larry,
And if he'd learn to speak,
He'll be well wicked as Prince Harry.
Oh, he'll soon put the spanner up Branagh,
However Kenny jostles for first place,
And Simon Callow – don't be silly,
All he does is show off his . . .
No, arise, arise, Sir Jase!

It's going to be Jason Donovan.
On Jason shall descend the muse of fire.
When gifts that god-like mingle
It makes your nipples tingle
And, face the fact, Sir Laurence never made a decent single.
Oh, they clamoured when Cher played King Richard –

Now *there*'s a show I simply couldn't face:
Cher was better, for my money,
Singing lovely songs with Sonny.
No, arise, arise, Sir Jase!

We know Donald Sinden's quite desperate,
But think what we might be beginning –
The audience in fear of Sir Donald as King Lear
More Sinden against than sinning.

No, it's going to be Jason Donovan.
It's Jason who has brushed Apollo's lyre.
Sir Laurence got the show when he did *Time*, I know,
But *Sealed with a Kiss* –

That's what I call a video.
McKellen may know Shakespeare backwards . . .
And do it, given half an inch of space,
But after causing all that trouble
For that boring pile of rubble,
No, arise, arise, Sir Jase

. . . and Lady Kylie!
Arise, arise, Sir Jase!

JEREMY HARDY

There, that's better. Well, my name is Jeremy Hardy, since you ask. And I make no bones about it – I was brought up in Surrey. There's no point beating around the bush. Social deprivation played no part in my upbringing whatsoever. If any kids went barefoot down my street it was because their parents put Wilton carpet ouside on the pavement.

I do have a social life, in spite of what you might think. I've actually got a friend called Steve. I suppose most people have, really, it's nothing to brag about, but he means a lot to me. Steve's a bit disorganized – he is an untogether unit. I remember one time he was staying with me, and when I woke up in the morning he was already meddling, fiddling, around the flat. I could hear him walking around the flat, and he came into my room and he said, 'Oh Jeremy, I've used your toothbrush, I hope you don't mind.'

And I said, 'Well, actually, Steven, yes, I do mind. I think it's rude of you. You might have asked me first. For all I know you've got some gum disease, plaque and pulsar . . . something like that.'

He said, 'No, no. It's all right, I used it to clean some dog shit off my shoe.'

So we got dressed, and we went up to Camden Lock market, which is an antiques market in North London. We were looking round the stalls, and the minute my back was turned Steve disappeared. He vanished. And then he came bounding up to me, pleased as Punch, and said, 'Jeremy, look what I've got for fifteen quid. Art Deco chocolate.'

I said, 'Steven, this is Toblerone.'

When I'm travelling on the Underground in London and there aren't very many seats and the sliding doors open and a couple get on, I

won't move to another seat in order to allow that couple to sit together. I'm sorry, why should they? What possible good will it do them? To some couples it seems important to be seen to sit together publicly and manifest their oneness to a compartment by intertwining bits of themselves. And no one's impressed. We're not sitting there thinking, blast, I won't be able to hold hands with either of those two then. Just my luck. I can't abide couples like that. The sort of people who live together but go down the pub for a snog. Eat the same Twiglet from opposite ends and meet. Girlfriends in their boyfriends' rugby shirts with the collars turned up. Why do people do this? Have they got pimples on their necks they're embarrassed about? Has the love bite gone septic or what? Actually, a love bite's a disgusting thing to do to another human being to show them that you care. You might as well whack them in the neck with a steak tenderizer, put a heart on their forehead with a branding iron.

This is one of my snappiest suits that I'm sporting because it is being televised. I didn't actually pay for this. I got this in return for sexual favours. I went to Boots on my brother's behalf. But I'll admit I'm quite a pallid unit. I'm a bit wan because there hasn't been much sun this year, but I don't cheat with lamps and creams. I don't fake tans. I think I might Tippex my abdomen to make the rest of me look darker.

I'm going to finish now, but before I do there's something that's on my mind because it's been on yours, and I know this: you've been sitting there thinking, well, here's a charming, erudite bit of a swinging sex machine, and you've been impressed by me, but you're thinking, he's a bit of a small bastard, isn't he? Particularly the people up in the balcony. They're looking down. They're thinking, he's a runt, he's a small little bastard. I know that's what you're thinking. In actual fact, I'm not actually that small because, in proportion to the size of my genitals, I'm quite big.

My name is Jeremy Hardy, and goodnight to you.

Bed Sketch

*An actor and an actress are in bed together. Trevor, the director, and
a second actor watch them.*

ACTRESS: How . . . um . . . was it for you?

ACTOR 1: It was terrific. How was it for you?

ACTRESS: Amazing. Great. How was it for you, Trevor?

TREVOR: It was fine. It was lovely. You're really smashing, super,
clever actors. Well, I think we've rehearsed the foreplay part well
enough now. Let's move on to the bit that involves the sexual
climax, shall we, darling? So, sweetheart, from you I want a long,
convincing orgasm. OK? OK . . . and go.

ACTRESS: (*Actor 1 moves on top of actress*) Oh, no. Yippee! Hurrah!
Tally ho! Yikes! Crumbs!

TREVOR: Darling, what was that?

ACTRESS: Well, an orgasm.

TREVOR: That's how you think an orgasm sounds?

ACTRESS: God, this is really embarrassing. You see . . . um . . . I've
never actually . . . had . . . an orgasm. Well, a friend of mine had
one, at least she thinks she did, last April. I mean, I could ring her
up and ask her.

ACTOR 1: Perhaps I could be of some assistance here?

TREVOR: Please do, love.

ACTOR 1: Obviously in my time I've heard lots of female orgasms.
Sure . . . And they normally sound like this . . . (*Very long yawn.*)

TREVOR: That's a yawn, love.

ACTOR 2: Listen, I'll tell you what a female orgasm sounds like.
Listen.

TREVOR: Yep.
ACTOR 2: Everyone knows, a female orgasm sounds like this . . . (*Bed-springing noise.*)
TREVOR: That's the bed!
ACTOR 1: Oh, it's the bed.

(*Enter Stavros.*)

STAVROS: Donna be stupe. The female orgasm sound like this. *Baaaah!*

Woke up this morning, I was folding my bed back into a couch. I almost broke both my arms because it's not one of those kind of beds.

Hermits have no peer pressure. It's a good thing to say to the police next time they stop you.
  'Licence and registration, please.'
  'Hermits have no peer pressure.'
  'Licence and registration, please.'
  'Whenever I think about the past it just brings back so many memories.'
  'Licence and registration, please.'
  'There's a fine line between fishing and just standing on the shore like an idiot.'
  'Licence and registration, please.'
  'What's another word for "thesaurus"?'
  See the cop start crying. STEVEN WRIGHT

JOHN WELLS

Dear Bill

Ah, good evening. Only a few more hours to go and the nation goes to the urns for its tryst with destiny. I don't know how you feel. I'm absolutely bloody knackered. I mean, in the old days before the terrorist bazooka, it used to be quite fun mingling with the hoi polloi. You always had one lobbing an egg or pouring treacle down your neck. It was quite jolly. Now that only the faithful are allowed within mortar range of the boss, it's more like being in *The Mousetrap*. You're actually stuffed – everyone wishes you were – and after a run as long as ours is, everyone knows who did it.

I don't know whether you've been to one of Margaret's Nuremberg-style rallies? They're all organized by this little sky pilot, co-friend of Ronnie Reagan's, Hopalong Cassidy, works for Billy Graham – I think his name is Barlow. Anyway, he was Billy Graham's fall-out man, and really it was a frightful shock to the party faithful because in the old days it was a few jars in the snug, then bundle down to the village hall for the big speech. Now they have to be on parade in the local conference centre twelve hours before curtain-up, stone-cold sober. Then the warm-up man comes on with his little gag book, makes them all shake hands, practise laughing and sharing, and works them into a fantastic frenzy. Then zero hour minus one, strobe lighting, disorientation techniques, ghastly music by that awful little hairy chimpanzee who made so much money out of interfering with cats. By the time the royal party gets on the stage, they're absolutely frothing at the mouth, waving their flags, wetting themselves and don't know where they are. Which, if you've heard some of Margaret's jokes, is a very good thing really. Doesn't matter to them breaking the furniture laughing, climbing over each other, and when Margaret starts waving her flag, they go positively ape-shit. The night I was there, they actually had to turn the sprinklers on. I was quite grateful for the SAS, really: otherwise we'd have all been stripped to the buff.

You've got all this showbiz razzmatazz, actually, from the smelly socks, the other side. I don't know whether you've seen it, but these Wardour Street spivs are trying to present the image of the little pillock as a sort of balding Rambo from the valleys. Well, the general idea is, you see, you tell Mr Silly Billy and Hattersley and Co. to bugger off and leave the stage to Super-Ginge who, in the company of a few carefully selected relatives, is seen to soar above the sordid realities of Labour life on the wings of Welsh song.

I don't know whether you've seen ours, provided by the Corsican brothers Saatchi and Saatchi, but pretty duff ads, in my view. There's Luigi Saatchi dressed up as a conjuror doing something disgusting with a pantomime horse. Then Margaret comes on, lot of old film of Margaret mingling with the mighty, i.e. shaking hands with Hoppo, eleven wogs and then Hoppo again. I think the thing is, they see Margaret's really star card as the fact that she's the only British politician the poor old gunslinger can recognize. That's why they're tramping her off, you probably saw, to go and have 'our' photograph taken with him in a gondola in that ghastly Italian sewage farm. The time I went there, stepped out of the hotel, fell straight in the swimming pool.

It's rather hard luck on Batman and Robin. They seem to have vanished into that orifice into which the Woosnam bird was last seen disappearing. Apparently after the show is over, Dr Death is joining our lot, and that little Scotch fellow is going back to the Borders to commune more closely with the sheep-sheds of the Falklands. I don't know whether in truth we've actually got 40 per cent of the polls, but it's a really triumphant trick getting the little bugger Mark back over to America. If he was still here, we'd be lagging very badly. Margaret was hoping to play a final trump card by announcing on the eve of the poll that she was hoping to be a grandmother. Miss Bergahof pregnant. Given the boy Mark's sense of direction, I think it's highly unlikely.

Vote Labour, vote Labour. Good luck to you all.

Fills in for a Back-stage Cock-up

It's so fucking embarrassing, isn't it? Have you ever done that? Have you ever worked your bollocks off trying to put on a small, light family entertainment, and then two artists that you thought were friends decided it would be amusing to get pissed instead of going on and doing a carefully rehearsed sketch? It's happening to me all the time. It's very embarrassing. However, perhaps, just as some kind of recompense for my two dearest ex-friends who are about to come on, as the curtain rises – perhaps we could just rehearse this – as the curtain rises, just the word 'bollocks' shouted quite firmly. Can I just rehearse you in this? 3–2–1 . . . *BOLLOCKS!*

Thank you. That's fine. I think that might surprise them into something. Meanwhile you can imagine there's a scene of serenity and peace backstage. Trickles of blood are about to appear down each side. Little thumping noises and so on. I see one of my friends now on the right-hand stage, the other one on the left. I think we may be quite soon ready to go. Is that correct? No, no, shaking heads and so forth.

So, a little about the genesis of the sketch you're about to see. It's called simply 'Who Killed Maureen?' and is set on one of the South Sea islands in 1926. The story concerns a colonial governor called Augusta and her husband Jane. We begin the sketch on a summer's afternoon with the colonial governor reading *The Times*. Dot, dot, dot . . . dot, dot, dot . . . dot to the power of twenty-five.

Have you ever pondered, as I have many times, on the similarity of a pelican and British Gas? They can both stick their bills up their arses. Incidentally, incidentally, Bloody Ghastly, isn't it, this BG? What is that about? Beautiful Globe, this sort of pathetic way advertisers have suddenly seen there's a green bandwagon and they've chased after it. British Gas stands for Beautiful Globe. If anyone would like to leave behind a slip of paper on which the initials BG better express British Gas, I should be very, very grateful.

The other thing I was going to ask you if you've ever done is this: have you ever appeared on stage to fill in rather quietly for some friends and then suddenly had this extraordinary desire to urinate? Again, that's something else always happening to me.

The twenty-fourth of August 1957 saw a very exciting moment for my mother. It was my birth. Moving swiftly on through kindergarten, prep school, summary dismissals and expulsions, I arrived at man's estate at the age of eighteen or nineteen, like most of us did. And I said to myself, this globe, this earth, what is it here for? Who put it there? What is God really about? Some people, when speaking about AIDS, have said that AIDS is a punishment from God for abhorrent or promiscuous lifestyles. I would like us to consider what kind of God could look down on an earth which daily rehearses millions of acts of brutal, pitiless cruelty and horror and ignores them and instead visits the foulest plague ever to have been given to humankind on those whose only sin is to slip between the sheets with those they like. What kind of God would do that? No kind of God. AIDS is not a judgement on its victims; it's a judgement on those who pass by on the other side.

Well, we're now ready, I think, for some more action. Thank you for this frank talk. I've enjoyed it very much. And I've rather fallen in love with you and decided perhaps to give up my celibacy because there are one or two people here I'd rather like to go to bed with. So see you all later in my dressing room. Goodbye.

78 ☆ JOSIE LAWRENCE AND RICHARD VRANCH

'Tired and Emotional'

Now you've gone all that remains
Is a memory,
Like when you took me to the
Cup Final at Wembley.
Now our love match is over and done,
And you've won,
Though I tried —
Now I'm tired and emotional.

Don't worry, darling,
I know that I'll get by.
I'm sorry for ripping your clothes,
And also your black eye.
Please try to understand I was mad —
You're a cad.
Damn your hide!
I'm so tired and emotional.

I walk around
From room to room,
And your presence is still there.
It lingers on,
Like the perfume
Of your smelly underwear
That I still keep there
On the bedroom chair.
I dream of how
It might have been

If our love affair had lasted,
But now I'm tired and emotional,
Darling,
And I think that you are
Such a rotten bastard.

Used to be a time when I'd think,
He adores me,
Till I overheard you telling
A friend, 'Oh she bores me.'
Now I sit alone with a bottle
Of rum,
Feeling numb.
I'm pie-eyed,
Also tired and emotional.

Oh, woe is me!
Oh, lonely me!
What am I to do?
I can't go on with this misery,
When I know it's true.
Boo hoo hoo hoo
Hoo hoo hoo hoo.
No one else could . . .

(*She stops, cries and rubs her
face, smearing lipstick and
mascara all over herself, then
composes herself and re-starts pianist.*)

No one else could ever take
Your place, dear,
Though right now I'd like to
Smash your face, dear.
I'd love to get down on my
Hands and knees
And beg you to stay
And not go away.

Don't leave me, please don't
Leave me.
(*Pause. She cries.*)

But I've still got my pride,
And anyway I'm too tired
And emotional.
Yes, I'm far too tired,
Tired and
Emotional.

(*Cries. Gestures to audience
not to applaud.*)

MIKE McSHANE AND TONY SLATTERY

Brief Encounter

TONY: (*Pacing*) It's no good. I can't bear the pretence any longer. I feel so guilty and sordid and ghastly and dirty and ghastly and ghastly and ghastly. I must tell her now. (*Calls into wings*) Amanda! Come here, darling!

(*Mike enters in ballgown.*)

MIKE: What *is* it Elyot, my love? Gracious, it's cold. Shall I poke the fire?

TONY: There isn't time. Darling, I feel so sordid and dirty and ghastly and beastly and dirty and ghastly and dirty and sordid and ghastly and dirty and dirty and dirty.

MIKE: Then you must wash.

TONY: Don't make fun!

MIKE: I'm not. You really smell. But it doesn't matter. I still love you.

TONY: I know. And that's what makes this harder.

MIKE: OK, but don't grab my hair.

TONY: No, darling, you don't understand. I want to go it alone.

MIKE: That's all right. I'll sit and watch.

TONY: *No*, darling. I . . .

MIKE: Calm down, Elyot! You've slipped into a blue funk.

TONY: Yes! And it's one that can't be wiped up. The brutal fact is . . . I'm leaving you.

(*Pause. Mike suddenly goes into bad American Cockney.*)

MIKE: 'Ere's a to do an' *no* error! Lawks a mussy, wiv you bein' as such like in chim chim cheroo, garn, guv'nor, at tuppence a bag!

TONY: Amanda, you can't avoid the issue just by talking bollocks.

MIKE: But you used to be so *amused* by my Dick Van Dyke impersonation! Elyot, what sort of woman do you want me to be? Just tell me and I'll be it. Beguiling? (*He makes face.*) Athletic? (*He skips.*) Rod Steiger? ('You're coming to the party, missy. No one makes fun of Judd Fry.') Mysterious? (*He puts his dress sleeve over his face.*)

TONY: Go back to Rod Steiger.

MIKE: So you're a homicide detective, Mr Tibbs . . .

TONY: Stop it, stop it! Don't you see what it takes to make a marriage? It takes commitment, honesty, bauxite.

MIKE: Who needs bauxite? We were in *love*!

TONY: Love is a messy business.

MIKE: We can always put more towels down. Elyot, we used to be so happy. So happy and lovely and happy and lovely. Shall I put on some music? (*He puts gramophone on head. Top flips open and music plays.*)

MIKE: (*Moves to behind Tony and puts his arms around him.*) Do you remember Venice?

TONY: How could I forget! (*They embrace.*) Venice! Our wedding night!

(*They dance.*)

MIKE: How we kissed! It took six gondoliers to remove your tongue from my throat.

TONY: Yes! Your nipples stood out like Bakelite bullets.

MIKE: And the gypsy band! I danced through the night.

MIKE: It slipped my mind.

TONY: But that was *then*, and this is *now*! (*He throws Mike aside.*) I've been living a *lie*. It's been hanging over me like an old man's unusually dangly conker bag. I've been unfaithful, darling. I never meant to hurt you.

MIKE: Hurt me? Hurt me? (*Laughs hysterically.*) You could never hurt *me*, shrimp-dick! I hope you used protection.

TONY: Yes. Rubber johnnies. Well, I say rubber. In fact, they were Art Deco. Made of Clarice Cliffe pottery. In the shape of Nancy Mitford.

MIKE: This woman, who is she?

TONY: Not *she*, darling: *they*!

MIKE: It's all right, darling! I forgive you. I . . . I'd just like to know their names.

TONY: Clarissa.

MIKE: I forgive you. And?

TONY: And Mabel.

MIKE: I forgive you. And?

TONY: And Roger.

MIKE: I forgive you.

TONY: And Shergar.

MIKE: I forgive you.

TONY: . . . Bonnie Langford.

MIKE: (*Walks over to Tony and strokes his face.*) You complete bastard! (*He knees Tony in groin.*)

My favourite chair is a wicker chair. It's my favourite chair because I stole it. I was at a party, a very crowded party, and when no one was looking I went over to it and I unravelled it and stuck it through the keyhole in the door. The girl who was in it was almost killed.

My girlfriend hates it when we take a bath together and I practise skipping rocks.

STEVEN WRIGHT

NIGEL PLANER

Nicholas Craig

I'd like to talk to you tonight about 'Acting'. The art of 'Acting', or the craft, if you so wish – don't let's start tearing each other to pieces over that one before we've even begun.

Acting is like climbing Mount Everest in the dark with a shark on your back, and when you get to the summit you find you have to ski down the other side, in your pyjamas, without falling over, or you'll be shot and eaten by jackals. Of course, it's heaven on bloody toast when you get it right, isn't it?

I don't know how far we are going to get tonight in the allotted time – we may unleash the slavering beast of Thespis. Here I am, a lectern and a pair of slacks, but in performance terms we are sitting on a volcano. So fasten your seatbelts: it's going to be a bumpy night.

Why do Actors act? Why do we need them to act? Do they, in fact, 'act' at all? Or just stand around in nice costumes and shout a lot? You see, it's not just a question of learning one's lines and saying them. No, no. The Actor has a duty, in rehearsals, to dig and trawl and dredge a text for every last calorie of emotional nutrition, be he in Shakespeare, be he in Coward, be he in Cooney.

Take a line like this one: 'My dear Algie, I thought you were down in Shropshire. How ripping to find that you're up instead.' A very simple line . . . or is it? What's it like to have a friend called Algie? Ask around. Better still, look through the phone book, find someone called Algie, get to know him, befriend him. Go to Shropshire, find out why it's so ripping *not* to be there. Live the line.

You see, the audience haven't paid just to have a nice night out. No, they want gut-wrenching primal thrillingness. They want the truth. They want the Text. We cannot go back to it often enough. The Text,

the text, the text. Eat it, sleep it, love it. Take it to the Caprice for supper – something rather lovely might happen. The text the text the text text text text text text text text . . . Shall we all say that? Text text text text text text text . . . Now, how are we going to get this?

Rehearsals, you see, are very much the life blood of the Actor. They're where we reveal our spiritual nudity to each other. Quite honestly, I'd be happy to do nothing but rehearse for the rest of my days. Make no mistake, the rehearsal room is no place for the faint-hearted. You need strength to carry on after lunch when the crossword's only a quarter done; you need stamina to go on when the coffee's run out and the workmen are drilling outside; you need animal determination, guts, self-belief; and if you're playing the leading role, you need to make a cheesecake to prove that you're not starry or grand or anything.

What is it that makes Actors so special? Well, in addition to Olympic fitness, supreme powers of concentration, the acceleration of a puma and an enormous appetite for just sheer bloody sweat and grind and just plain bloody old-fashioned hard work, the Actor has to have an almost supernatural ability to . . . to 'other be'. Now, OK, 'other be', 'other be' – what is 'other be'? Well, in the words of Peter Brook, the guru of International Theatre, the Actor has to be a sort of 'magician-poet-shaman-warrior-priest', whichever medium he is in. It doesn't matter if it's telly, commercials, theatre, crime re-enactments, industrial training videos or dressing up as Mr Kia Ora at the Ideal Home Exhibition – the same rules apply. Nigel Havers brings as much emotional fire-power to a Lloyds Bank ad as he does to an episode of *Bergerac*. So, to me, there's no conflict between acting in commercials and the kind of serious, classical acting which wins one awards at the Barbican and the National.

Now, I suppose I should say here, about the award . . . I mean, obviously, as an Actor every fibre of one's being is utterly revolted by the very notion of awards. It's not a competition, is it? So to see it engraved in bronze that one is a better Actor than say, Charlie Dance – I mean, it doesn't actually say that on the award, but that effectively is what it means – is not only very, very silly but also hideously embarrassing for both Charlie and myself. I mean, I've seen Charlie be bloody good in some things – I'm sure we all have. No, he's a smashing actor. Love him to death. And also a bloody good mate. Nevertheless, there's no point in pretending that I haven't won the bloody thing because I have. And no matter how much I try and conceal it behind invitation cards, there it is: 'Best Actor in Hitherto Unperformed Late Jacobean Tragedy'.

You know, one of the saddest sights I think I ever saw, was Charlie Dance coming out of Maxim's in Paris and getting into a white Rolls-Royce. I thought, You silly, silly, silly, silly man, what are you doing? You could be playing Justice Shallow at Leatherhead, doing some proper acting for a change. But then these things happen, don't they, when people believe their own publicity. Sad but unavoidable. He has had a rotten trot workwise though, hasn't he? It is awful, unemployment. Only last week Jeremy Irons tried to sell me his BMW, poor sausage. Anthony Andrews has had time this summer to repave his entire patio. Slapped wrists, though, Craig. I'm fortunate, of course, at the moment for being in the position of having too much work, which is lovely.

As you probably know, I'm doing an Atrocitus at the RSC at the moment. The make-up alone is nearly killing me – I have to be at the theatre fourteen hours before a performance, and sometimes, if we have a matinée the next day, I have to scrub off and start putting the new make-up on before the evening show is even over. It's a nightmare. And then there's this, and the novel, and the dry skiing lessons . . . I mean, no sane person would undertake a workload like this, surely? Actor trying to stay ever so slightly sane in here.

Well, thank you for coming with me on this journey . . . this place . . . my home . . . these . . . boards, quivering with the resonations of actors through the centuries: Irving, Burbage, Keen, Peter Barkworth. This is where we do it: the stage door with its fluttering notice boards, the corridor heavy with the aroma of sweat and grease paint, the taut ropes stretching into the flies, the prop table groaning with leather and buckles and whips and those spiky ball-on-chain things.

> Stern and bulbous stand the wig blocks,
> Harsh the spirit gum,
> Putty in the make-up box
> For noses yet to come.

A bank of telemessages,
A furry pig from Sue,
A plate of curling sandwiches,
Chrysanths from you-know-who.

And it's out through the door at 'Beginners, please',
And it's 'Good luck, Bill,' and it's trembling knees,
And it's down the dark stairs in the wings to wait,
And it's fear and big hugs and a minute to eight.

Oh, when will it end, this exquisite pain?
When can we all do kissing again?
Then the voice of a dresser rallies the ranks:
'Did you get my card?', 'Got a fag?', 'Ooh, thanks.'
Oh, why do I trade in these freezing church halls?
Why do I suffer these ten o'clock calls?
Why do I sweat through an inch of Max Factor?
Because, lovey, you're a fucking Actor!

World peace is possible if Actors want it!

Bought some land. It was kind of cheap. It was on somebody else's property.

Bought an ant farm. I don't know where I'm gonna get tractors that small.

Bought a cordless extension cord.

Bought a decaffeinated coffee table. Can't even tell by looking at it. STEVEN WRIGHT

ROWAN ATKINSON AND ELTON JOHN

Intelligent Interview

ROWAN: (*In pedantic, crusty tone*) Good evening and welcome to the National Theatre Platform, where we are in the middle of our series of very informal chats with major performers. It has been a very exciting series, which has so far taken in such performing giants as Sir Ian McKellen, Dame Judi Dench and, of course, Christopher Biggins, but tonight, I'm particularly glad to welcome a young man who is certainly no giant, but has made a huge impression in his chosen field. Ladies and gentlemen – Mr Elton John.

(*Elton enters. Huge applause.*)

ROWAN: Elton – do you mind if I call you Elton?

ELTON: No.

ROWAN: Well, 'Elton', obviously the first question everybody wants to ask you is – funny name, Elton. How did you come up with it?

ELTON: A friend of mine knew someone called Elton, and I just kind of liked it.

ROWAN: Great. Did you ever consider John Elton?

ELTON: No, I didn't.

ROWAN: Fine. So, let's go back to those early albums. Your first was, I believe, just called *Elton John*.

ELTON: That's right.

ROWAN: And you didn't feel awkward with the name? You didn't feel that people would say, 'Wait a minute – what a bloody stupid name. He means John Elton. They've gone and cocked up the sleeve and printed the bloody name the wrong way round'?

ELTON: No, it sounded great to me. And, frankly, I thought people would be more interested in the music than the name.

ROWAN: Perhaps . . . Now, going back to the songs themselves – the lyrics were written by Bernie Taupin.

ELTON: That's right.

ROWAN: Well, I'd like to talk about Bernie for a while, since obviously he's been an enormous influence on your career.

ELTON: Yes.

ROWAN: Did you ever think about getting him to change his name? Because, obviously, Taupin Bernie would have been more consistent with Elton John.

ELTON: Look, do you want to talk about the music on those early albums or not?

ROWAN: Absolutely. I'd love to. 'Your Song' is a classic, isn't it?

ELTON: (*Modestly*) Well, it's quite popular.

ROWAN: Now, in one wonderful, informal verse in that song, talking about the eyes of the person the song's about, you say: 'Excuse me for asking / But these things I do – / You see, I've forgotten / If they're green or they're blue.'

ELTON: Yes.

ROWAN: What I need to know is – is it this sort of chronic forgetfulness

that led you to forget that Elton isn't, in fact, a Christian name at all? It's a surname and not a very attractive one at that.

ELTON: No, really, let's talk about something else.

ROWAN: All right. Elton, let's talk about being a stage performer. Do you ever watch other performers and get jealous?

ELTON: I don't think so. Who do you mean?

ROWAN: Well, for instance, Ben Elton – in his case, the 'Elton' is in the right position – do you ever watch Ben and say, 'I wish I'd got my bloody name the right way round'?

ELTON: No, I don't.

ROWAN: Fair enough. Moving on – many consider your masterpiece to be the album *Goodbye, Yellow Brick Road*, and there's one song that people are particularly moved by, 'Candle in the Wind'.

ELTON: Yes, it's a lot of people's favourite.

ROWAN: This is actually a song dedicated to Norma Jean Baker, who changed her name to Monroe Marilyn.

ELTON: Marilyn Monroe.

ROWAN: My point exactly! Marilyn is a Christian name, so it comes first! Can't you see that? Are you word-blind, or what?

ELTON: All right – I've had enough of this.

ROWAN: No, wait, wait. Now, final question: you've achieved enormous success over the years, but, in fact, your first-ever solo British Number One came last year with 'Sacrifice'. Now, my big question is this: do you think you would have had to wait so long for a Number One if it hadn't been for your obviously mad, pointless name?

(*Elton draws a gun and shoots Rowan.*)

ELTON: What a head-dick.

I'*ve been arrested several times, once for resist-ing arrest.*
'*You're under arrest.*'
'*No, I'm not.*'
'*You're under arrest.*'

I *was arrested for walking in someone else's sleep.*
'*What are you doing here?*'
'*Nothing, just browsing.*'   STEVEN WRIGHT

BEN ELTON

I thought it might be a little apt, at this stage in the evening, to discuss the subject of contraception. And the sexism therein. Because I don't know who it was that designed all the various methods of contraception available to the public, but I hazard a guess that it was a man.

Let us take a look at a consumer's guide to contraception. On the girls' side, for the women, there are three options. You can have a little pill that might give you thrombosis, heart failure, and mess up your skin. Lovely, lovely, lovely.

Or the lady in question may choose to favour a little rubber pudding basin, which she is expected to fill with spermicidal napalm (*squelch squelch squelch*).

Really gets you in the mood for a shag that, doesn't it, eh? You're thinking, *Oh dear, this stuff kills six million sperms – what's it doing to the inside of my fanny then?* You'd have to think! You'd have to wonder! It's not an aphrodisiac – the Dutch cap does not turn you on. I mean, 'Oh, God, do we have to shag tonight? I don't wanna put . . . Oh, all right then. Stay out of the bathroom. You won't like this.' You stagger into the bathroom. It's midnight. You've got work in the morning. Dig out the old Dutch cap, fill it up with napalm (*squelch squelch squelch*). *Think I'd better put the whole tube in. I don't want to get pregnant by him.* You're half pissed, one Pernod too many, and you're trying to guide this up you. The bathroom's spinning round, you've forgotten to take your knickers off, you can't – *argh* . . . You can see three gussets. You don't know which one to aim at, you know?

This is prior to making love. You've got napalm dribbling down your thighs. Bung your leg up on the toilet to steady yourself a little bit. You're trying to guide it in. You can hear him snoring next door. You think, *I'm gonna wake that bastard up and I'll make him shag me if I have to put it in a splint after going through this.* You're trying to stick it in and you don't know whether you've got the right position or not, 'cos I've never met a girl who was sure: 'Well, my fanny doesn't look a bit like the diagram at the clinic, I can tell you.' And she finally ... *oop* ... it's in position ... it's there ... it's ... oh, no! It shoots across the bathroom. You're shouting, 'Have another fag! It's gone behind the toilet!' Trying to fish it out – *Oh dear, I must clean that bog.* You fish it out from behind and you're picking the pubes off. You think, *They might be mine, but I'm not sticking them back up again, am I?* You get up, you fill it up with napalm again (*squelch*), rinse it under the tap first, fill it ... *Oh, bollocks, I put Colgate in it!* Try and work out whether fluoride has the same effect on sperm as it has on plaque – *Jeez, what did I just brush my teeth with?*

You know, I've been there. I'm a bit of a new man. I make an effort. I try. You know: 'Is there anything I can do to help, love?'

'Just catch it!'

'Whooah! There we go!' I've caught a few shooting across the bathroom. Peter Shilton, me. 'Whey! There we go!' They ought to train goalkeepers like that. Give a whole new meaning to the term 'capped for England', wouldn't it?

Or the lady might say, 'No, I don't want the rubber pudding basin. I prefer to have a small piece of barbed wire stuffed up me flaps.'

That is what is available for the girls, right? You've got thrombosis, napalm or barbed wire. Now, what has medical science, in all its genius, come up with for the boys?

Rubber johnny! 'Well, it stops the ... Well, it works, rubber johnny!' Don't believe all those articles about the male pill. What is actually *there*? Rubber johnny. No decades of research into the hormonal balance of a man's body – no! No question of sticking a small fishhook down the one eye. Fuck all that – no! Rubber johnny! And, amazingly, lads offered this fabulous option – don't mess up your body, don't have any pain, just cover it up – still don't wanna do it. *I don't wanna use a rubber johnny. I don't like them. I don't like rubber johnnies. I don't wanna ... I'm sensitive. It spoils my sensitiv-*

ity 'cos I love you, darling, and I want to feel with us together in our . . . I'm sensitive, and I don't like it. I don't like rubber johnnies because I love you, and I'm a sensitive person – so stick a bit of barbed wire in your box, love, go on!

Ladies and gentlemen, it's a great pleasure to be here tonight. What we're raising tonight, consciousness, money, such important things. We know there's a crisis coming. We'll face it together. It needs a healthy National Health Service as well as evenings like this. Ladies and gentlemen, it's a real pleasure to be here. Thank you. My name's Ben Elton. Goodnight!

*C*an't wait to be arrested and go all the way to the witness stand.

'Do you swear to tell the whole truth and nothing but the truth, so help you God?'

'Yes. You're ugly. See that woman in the jury? I'd really like to sleep with her. Should I keep going, or are you going to ask me questions?'

I took a lie-detector test. No, I didn't.
STEVEN WRIGHT

'Burn, Burn, Burn, Burn, Burn'

The Conservative MP for Spelthorne, Surrey,
Has crowned his hitherto negligible career
Rescuing Great Britain from the moral slurry
In which it floundered up until this year.
The Conservative MP for Spelthorne, Surrey,
Moved the parliamentary debate
Which adorned our mighty nation
With that jewel of legislation
The Local Government Bill, Sub-section 28.

Burn, burn, burn, burn, burn the faggots!
We're standing with out backs against the wall.
Since school I couldn't stick 'em,
So now they're down let's kick 'em
Lest conscience make Noel Cowards of us all.
Britain's problem, all those years,
Was simply Peter Pears,
So stop the rot before it's far too late.
Rise up in a body,
Ban Big Ears, ban Noddy.
The MP for Spelthorne, Surrey, welcomes Section 28.

Burn, burn, burn, burn, burn the faggots!
Since none of them are Tories, I'm quite sure
From this day forward we shall use
Victoria's family values
(Her grandson, Eddie Clarence, we'll ignore).
Throughout our sceptred land

Reading Rimbaud will be banned –
It's the other Rambo we should emulate.
Healthy, macho thugg'ry
Beats biting the rugg'ry:
The MP for Spelthorne, Surrey, welcomes Section 28.

We'll extol the pre-permissive hero,
The idols who were strong and tough and clean:
Cary Grant, Mountbatten and Navarro,
Errol Flyn, Rock Hudson and James Dean.

Burn, burn, burn, burn, burn the faggots!
Let's flush the Church of England out *en masse.*
Oh, sure, our Saviour moans
That we shall not throw stones –
I say thou shalt not covet thy neighbour's ass.
Human nature's how you fight it,
History's how you write it –
Alexander, Peter, Fred'rick weren't that great.
They're promiscuous as rabbits:
We deplore their filthy habits
(do we not, Cecil? . . . Hear, hear . . . Parkinson agrees).
The MP for Spelthorne, Surrey, welcomes Section 28.

Burn, burn, burn, burn, burn the faggots!
Backbenchers need a platform we can use.
With prejudice to fuel
We shall divide and rule –
Then afterwards we can get down to the Jews.
So if you find your son
Has slit his wrists, well done!
He's lower than a reptile, so why worry?
For at the final judgement, who are Shakespeare or Fassbinder,
Homer and Tchaikovsky, Inigo Jones or Gide or Spender,
Satie, Saki, Williams, Wilde, Byron, Brooke and Laughton,
Plato, Auden, Burra, Caravaggio and Orton,
Bennett, Maugham, Colette, Nijinski, Strachey, Sophocles,
Michelangelo, Mishima, Horst, Praxiteles,

Marlowe, Forster, Rochester, Mann, Stein or Botticelli,
Lorca, Hockney, Woolf and Jean Genet, Verlaine and Shelley,
T. E. Lawrence, Leonardo, Proust and J. M. Barrie
To challenge me, the Conservative MP for Spelthorne, Surrey?

JOHN CLEESE AND TINA TURNER

JC: Every now and again, and it's rarely, a star is born. And less often that star becomes a superstar. Occasionally, once perhaps every three or four hundred years, such a superstar becomes a legend. And just once in the lifetime of each galaxy such a legend becomes a myth. A rarer journey still is that from myth to amateur cathedral swallower. It's my privilege tonight to introduce you to someone who has reached only the level of myth – 'Myth' Tina Turner.

(Enter Tina. There is a lot of kissing.)

JC: I'm sorry, we haven't met before. Miss Turner, may I be the very first to welcome you here this evening?

TT: John, please do call me Tina.

JC: Well, I'd rather not if you don't mind. It's such an awful name. I wonder, perhaps . . . can I call you Eric?

TT: All right.

JC: Eric, I hope you don't mind me asking this, but I notice that you have a slightly unusual accent. Are you, in fact, black at all?

TT: Yes, I am, in fact, black.

JC: Black.

TT: Black.

JC: Black, and a woman too. How absolutely splendid. And that is what you would like to talk about this evening?

TT: Well, we can, but actually I'm here to sing.

JC: Fine, fine. Why not? *(Asks backstage)* Is that all right? Ah, apparently there's an orchestra here. How fortunate. I thought we were going to have to discuss disadvantages. This is a microphone. If you sing in this end, you see, the ladies and gentlemen can hear you better. And it's probably better if you face them. Lots of teeth and smiles, and jolly good luck. They're absolutely behind you, so don't be nervous. They're very charitable, these charitable audiences. And one word of advice. While you're singing, if I may suggest, try and move around a bit, preferably in the rhythm of the music if possible, sort of 'Onward, Christian Soldiers'. (*Does silly dance.*)

TT: Actually John, I prefer to do something like . . . (*Struts about a bit.*)

JC: A word in your ear, Eric. People in this country don't like a show-off. So keep it a bit simple, OK? Less is more, that kind of thing. Now, what is the name of this sing that you're going to song for us?

TT: I'm going to song . . . I'm going to sing 'Steamy Windows'.

JC: 'Steamy . . .' Fine. Ladies and gentlemen, would you please listen with great politeness and patience to 'Steamy Widows', as sung by my absolutely best friend, Myth Eric Turner.

(*Tina Turner sings.*)

A Small Rewrite

There is a knock at the door.

PRODUCER: Come.

SHAKESPEARE: (*Clears throat.*)

PRODUCER: Bill, Bill, good to see you.

SHAKESPEARE: Sorry I was late. The traffic was a bitch.

PRODUCER: Good to see you. Well, the play's going well, isn't it? Looks like we've got a bit of a smash on our hands.

SHAKESPEARE: Well, it seems to be OK, yes.

PRODUCER: They all seem to go for the ones with the snappy titles. *Hamlet* – perfect.

SHAKESPEARE: Act 3 may be a bit long. I don't know.

PRODUCER: *Act 3* may be a bit long? In fact, generally, I think we've got a bit of a length problem.

SHAKESPEARE: Oh?

PRODUCER: It's five hours, Bill, on wooden seats and no toilets this side of the Thames.

SHAKESPEARE: Yes, well, I've always said the Rose Theatre is a dump, frankly. The sooner they knock it down and build something decent, the better.

PRODUCER: Exactly. So that's why I think we should trim some of the dead wood.

SHAKESPEARE: Dead wood?

PRODUCER: Yes, you know. Some of that stand-up stuff in the middle of the action.

SHAKESPEARE: You mean the soliloquies?

PRODUCER: Yes. And I think we both know which is the dodgy one.

SHAKESPEARE: Oh? Oh? Which *is* the dodgy one?

PRODUCER: To be ... nobler in the mind ... mortal coil, that one. It's boring, Bill. The crowd hates it. Yawnsville.

SHAKESPEARE: Well, that one happens to be my favourite, actually.

PRODUCER: Bill, you said that about the avocado monologue in *King Lear*. And the tap dance at the end of *Othello*. Be flexible.

SHAKESPEARE: Absolutely *not*. You cut one word of that, and I'm off the play.

PRODUCER: Bill, the king has got his costume change down to one minute. Hamlet's out there ranting on about God knows what in that soliloquy of yours, and Claudius is already in the wings waiting to come on with that very funny codpiece.

SHAKESPEARE: All right, why don't you cut the piece altogether?

PRODUCER: Bill, Bill, Bill, why do we have to fight? It's long, long, long. We could make it so snappy.

SHAKESPEARE: Snappy?

PRODUCER: Yes, you know, give it some pizzazz. How does it begin, that speech?

SHAKESPEARE: 'To be'.

PRODUCER: Come on, Bill.

SHAKESPEARE: 'To be a victim of all life's earthly woes or not to be a coward and take death by his proffered hand'.

PRODUCER: There, now, I'm sure we can get that down.

SHAKESPEARE: No, absolutely not. It's perfect.

PRODUCER: How about 'To be a victim or not to be a coward'?

SHAKESPEARE: It doesn't make sense, does it? To be a victim of what? To be a coward about what?

PRODUCER: OK, OK, take out 'victim', take out 'coward'. Just start 'To be or not to be'.

SHAKESPEARE: You can't say that. It's gibberish.

PRODUCER: But it's short, William. It's *short*. Listen to it – it flows. 'To be or not to be, that is the question.' Da da da da da da da da da da da.

SHAKESPEARE: You're damned right, it's the question. They won't have any bloody idea what he's talking about.

PRODUCER: OK, let's leave that and go on. Blah blah blah blah blah. 'Slings and arrows', good. Action, the crowds love it. 'Take arms', brilliant. 'Against those cursed doubts that do plague on man'.

Mmmm. Getting very woolly there, Bill. Plague's a bit tasteless at the moment. We'd have letters, actually. 'And set sail on a sea of troubles'. This is good. Travel – travel's very popular. So let's just take out the guff and see what we've got. 'To suffer the slings and arrows of outrageous fortune or to take arms against a sea of troubles'. Good.

SHAKESPEARE: Hmmn . . .

PRODUCER: Bill, it's brilliant.

SHAKESPEARE: It's absolute crap. What is he talking about? He's going to pull out a bow and arrow and potter down to the seaside. This is Prince Hamlet, not King Canute. Might as well kill himself if that's the best idea he can come up with.

PRODUCER: Creative thinking, Bill. Hamlet, perhaps he should top himself.

SHAKESPEARE: In Act I?

PRODUCER: Yes, well, look, we must think about bums on seats, Bill. Let's face it, it's the ghost that's selling this show at the moment. Joe Public loves the ghost. He loves the sword fights, he loves the crazy chick in the see-through dress who does the flower gags and then drowns herself. But no one likes Hamlet. No one.

SHAKESPEARE: All right, then, I'll kill him off for you. Ummm . . . 'Ay, there's the rub, to die, to sleep . . .' *Whoops*, Hamlet falls off the battlements.

PRODUCER: Bill, Bill, Bill. I can see you're annoyed. I'm sorry. Hamlet has his moments. The mad stuff is very funny. It really is hysterical. All I'm saying, Shaky, is that we could just shorten this one terribly dull speech.

SHAKESPEARE: All I'm saying is, no, you can't. One word and you can take my name off the credits.

PRODUCER: All right. I'll do you a deal. I'll trim this speech and you can put back in those awful Cockney grave diggers.

SHAKESPEARE: What, both of them?

PRODUCER: Yes.

SHAKESPEARE: And the skull routine?

PRODUCER: Yes, the whole sketch.

SHAKESPEARE: All right, then, you've got a deal. And we'll see which one history remembers.

PRODUCER: Bill, I love you . . . (*Aside*) Temperamental git.

KIT HOLLERBACH

Oh, God, I'm so nervous tonight. I mean, all the celebrities and stuff. An old college friend of mine once saw me. He said, 'Kit, the audience can smell fear.' He used to mess his pants as he walked on stage.

Oh, but this is so exciting. I remember when I first came to Great Britain. Where do you guys get off? *Great* Britain? Nobody else does this. You don't hear, like, Fab France. You know, sort of OK Czechoslovakia. I mean, before I came here I knew people wouldn't like me because I'm American. I don't know whether it's because of our, you know, invasion of several countries like Britain or whether it was because of the Waltons, but either way I thought to get around it I'd adopt an English accent, so I watched some black-and-white films in the States, and when I got off the train at Victoria, I went, 'Porter, I say, porter, have a care, my good man. That's my best hat box. I feel so wildly gay. Alec, I know you don't approve of women in public and neither do I. I'm so terribly, terribly, terribly sorry.' There wasn't an Alec or a porter, so I had to improvise with a couple of Belgian tourists. I never did make it to my hotel because every time I'd get in a taxi I'd go, 'Scotland Yard, and step on it, driver, there isn't a moment to lose.'

But I live here. God, I live with my English husband. By that I mean he eats pizza with a knife and fork. And sunburns under a 50-watt bulb. And is he *English*? He wears pyjamas with the top button done up and a tie. And he's useless. Like, I'll send him to the store to get some Tampax, not because I need them but just to humiliate him. He will get his own back – he'll return with six aubergines and a Twiglet. Honestly. And right now he's into body-building. Guys, you've got to be careful of this body-building stuff because what happens is your entire body gets puffed out, but your head remains exactly the same size. And this is to say nothing of your genitals.

Well, I've been out doing a little shopping today. I figure, you know, what the hell – a fool and his money are soon parted. That's why I spend Jeremy's. Oh, I like that joke. Humour me. But I figured I could get a lipstick. My girlfriend said to me, she says, 'You know, that lipstick does nothing for you.' I said, 'What do you want it to do? Take out the trash?' I feel naked without my lipstick. The trouble is, it takes me for ever to cover my body with it.

It's great to be here, you know. I come from a small town, Incline, Nevada. God, it is as American as British foreign policy, I tell you. But I've lived here a while. I have to say that I've made some observations about these people who live here, and, you know, I think sometimes the British people are too tolerant. I mean, how else would you explain hundreds of years of an inequitable class system and appliances that are sold without plugs? How can this be construed as an optional extra? And the class system – I'm sorry, it confuses me no end. I don't know how that works, you know. I'm starting to get an idea, though, that the higher class you are, the less consonants you use. So, like, 'Pass the wine' would be 'Pwaaaaaaaaaaaaaah.'

America is a lot simpler. We have two classes of people – people who say, 'Shit,' and people who say, 'Shiiiiit.' And, speaking of shit, you know, I don't like your Prime Minister. What's her name? Eva Thatcher Braun? This is a woman with the sensitivity of a dental hygienist. I've got nothing against Kinnock. I just think it's a shame her husband's such a spineless dork. Oh, come on, as a result of these two clowns – what is it? Section 28, the Alton bill, NHS, all this shit – I'm spending a lot of time marching in demonstrations. But I'm always careful not to clash with the police. I tend to wear neutral colours. Pastel tones.

Oh, look, I'm having too much fun. Surely this isn't right? I'm going to go home and watch some ads on TV. There's some soap-powder commercials I'm particularly keen to catch. I love these. The one where the woman complains ... She goes, 'Gosh, I just don't know what to do about these nasty blood stains on my husband's shirts.' If I were her, I'd ask a few questions. Or what

about the guy who's got blood, egg and sweat? What did he do, beat up a chicken?

Thank you very much.

I used to spend time with my grandfather when my mother was going to have another baby. She would send me out of the way, make me spend time with my grandfather, who was completely out of his mind, totally insane.

Every day he made us stand in a little room together, side by side, looking straight ahead for three minutes without talking to each other. He told me it was elevator practice.

Now some time I'll be in an elevator with someone. I'll say, 'Did your grandfather make you do this too?'

They'll say, 'What the hell are you talking about?'

My grandmother was also insane. She had pierced hearing aids. Unscented perfume ... came in a little empty bottle. One time she said, 'Steven, come over here. Here's $5 and don't tell your mother I'm giving this to you.'

I said, 'It'll cost you more than that.'

STEVEN WRIGHT

'A*llo! B*onjour, M*onsieur!*'

When I'm standing in ze street,
I say to all ze men I meet
'Allo! Bonjour, Monsieur!'
Per'aps eef eet's a sunny day,
I sit outside a small café –
'Allo! Bonjour, Monsieur!'
And mebbe eef a gentleman
Seems to want to 'old my hand
Why zen – c'est parfait!
After all, a girl must live!
And I've got lots of love to give
But I never forget to say . . .

Where is your johnny now, Johnny?
Don't be a tease!
Don't blame me if I don't want
A nasty disease.
It's a good tactic,
Just one prophylactic
In your pocket, just for luck;
So zo of me you're desirous,
Remember ze virus!
Before you're panic-struck.

At night I meet my artiste friends;
Ze fun and laughter never ends . . .
'Allo! Bonsoir, Monsieur!'
Oh, 'ow I love la vie Bohème –

I love each Gentilhomme ze same –
'Allo! Bonsoir, Monsieur!'
At 'eart, je suis une vagabonde;
And absinthe makes the 'eart grow fond . . .
So wiz some man I may make free . . .
But before I go wiz my beau-père,
I like to take a little care –
After all – zis is Gay Paree . . .

Where is your johnny now, Johnny?
Heavens above!
Wizout a little precaution, Johnny,
Let's not make love.
Just one little trickle
And I'm in a pickle –
It's no use to be contrite;
Maintenant c'est comme il faut,
For 'ow can I know
Who you were wiz last night?

Oh, zose halcyon days –
Life was lived in a haze –
And it's gone in a flash;
A cheeky bonjour – another amour –
And you woke wiz a rash;
To ze doctor for some pills, et c'était bien;
Alors, je ne regrette rien . . .

Where is your johnny now, Johnny?
Does it float on ze Seine?
Whatever you do wiz your johnny, Johnny,
Don't use it again.
If you are fond o' me,
Please use your condom, oui,
Extra strong to stop leaks;
So be a good fellow –
Use red, green or yellow
Put some colour in my cheeks.

Where is your johnny now, Johnny?
Don't be a clown!
Though we will 'ave lots of fun, Johnny,
There's no going down.
Before swapping saliva,
Don't be mean – spend a fiver!
You know you need not break ze bank;
For unless you're equipped,
You've got to stay zipped,
You'll have only yourself to thank.

So it's probably better
When you've got no French letter,
Yes, it's probably better to wank.

STEPHEN FRY

Yet Again

As the Sixties Tiller Girls leave the stage Stephen dances downstage, dressed in top hat, tails and fishnet tights.

Thank you, thank you, thank you, ladies and gentlemen. Thank you. It gives me several hot splashes of delight to welcome all of you to the wide world of *Hysteria 3!*

There is an extraordinary evening of comedy, entertainment, drama, music and dance lined up for you tonight on television, so it's all the kinder of you to be here at the London Palladium. No, I'm just being pointlessly lovely there.

But, certainly, welcome to the historic London Palladium. The poet Anthony Newley called this theatre – or, as we actors like to call it, for aggravating and irritating reasons, this 'space' – he called it 'The London Palladium. The P-A-L-L-adium, the super starry stadium that showbiz calls home'. So welcome to the home of showbiz – and, indeed, this theatre is a hive of history. I don't know who is sitting in J3 there, in the Grand Circle, the Royal Circle, but it was in that very seat, watching Su Pollard in *Babes in the Wood*, that the American author Thomas Harris – who wrote *Red Dragon* and *The Silence of the Lambs* – conceived the idea of the serial killer Dr Hannibal Lecter. So, sitting on a little bit of history there. What gave him the idea no one to this day quite knows.

And right up at the top there in B11 – perhaps of more historic significance – that's where, one dank, autumn afternoon, at a matinée of *Singing in the Rain*, Harry Secombe got the idea for 'Highway'. There's a little plaque if you look. The person behind you will be able to see it.

Perhaps the most famous seat of all is A17, which, I think, is down here somewhere. In A17, if you tilt your seat up, you can see there's a stain on the carpet, a rather unpleasant stain. This is connected to a man who was watching Jimmy Tarbuck doing one of his *Sunday Nights at the London Palladium*. And they do say that no matter how much you try to remove this awful thing, this ghastly, ghastly thing, it will always come back. The same, of course, is true of the stain on the carpet. I'm sorry, I may just have committed showbiz suicide there.

But that is enough theatre folklore. The last time we presented a *Hysteria!*, which for reasons too intricate and grotesque for the sane mind to grasp we called *Hysteria 2!*, there were two Berlins, two Germanies, Ceauşescu ruled in Romania, the most famous Gascoigne in England was Bamber and Margaret Thatcher ruled in 10 Downing Street. *Hysteria 2!* changed all that. And we're proud, if a little puzzled, to have wrought such extraordinary changes on the world stage. It's extraordinary, isn't it, that with a few amusing jokes and the sudden and unexpected use of the word 'clitoris', one can bring down dictators, ring up the Iron Curtain and end Margaret Thatcher's reign. But we also succeeded, and perhaps this was more broadly within the terms of our remit, in raising a great deal of money for people with AIDS.

Now this year *Hysteria!* – and those of you who are verbally minded might like to know that 'this year' is actually an anagram of 'hysteria': isn't that interesting? Yes, well, *quite* interesting. It's also an anagram of 'yif arse', but that will only mean something to you if you are a Norwegian pederast, and there aren't any in the audience, only two or three hundred at the most. But this year – 'hysteria' is also an anagram of 'hairy set', come to think of it, isn't it? And a partial anagram of 'kiss my shiny bott, Mr Waldegrave.' Very partial, I agree, but I don't think it can entirely be a coincidence. However, this year *Hysteria!* hopes to raise even more money.

A nice newspaper person – well, a newspaper person anyway – asked me the other day if the purpose of *Hysteria!* was to raise consciousnesses. This shows a fundamental misunderstanding of the purpose of *Hysteria!*, which has always been to have as much fun as is possible without the use of baby oil. Just one look around this auditorium shows me that your consciousnesses don't need raising. You know that there are hundreds of thousands of people dying of a dreadful disease, and you know that not enough is being done about it, and you are not above extending a brotherly or sisterly hand.

In a nation led by fools it becomes all of us to show that fellow feeling, mercy, tender regard are much more common human attributes than indifference and judgement. Some people might believe that decent, civilized values are best represented by intolerance, pitiless indifference. Some people might believe that decent, civilized human values are best represented by wishing to bring back hanging or being offended at the use of the word 'fuck'. Others believe decent, civilized human values reside best in kindliness, tenderness and delight. That's all. That's the *Hysteria!* philosophy. And I use the word 'philosophy' ... wrongly. But, as the Archbishop of Canterbury likes to say, 'That's enough tedious wank. Let's party!'

ALAN CUMMING, CRAIG FERGUSON, ROBERT LLEWELLYN, TONY SLATTERY

The Dissident

Three dinner-jacketed gentlemen are nursing champagne glasses and nibbly things on cocktail sticks.

MARTIN: David, you really have got to meet Sergiev Bolinski.

DAVID: My God! *The* Sergiev Bolinski? The novelist?

(David shakes hands with Bolinski.)

DAVID: My God, you're brilliant. I've read all your work. You're a genius.

SERGIEV: *(Soviet accent)* I pulsate with eager, rhythmic delight you should say so. Thank you.

DAVID: Sorry?

SERGIEV: I bulge with happiness. My head is purple and shiny.

DAVID: Your English is very . . . good.

SERGIEV: What?

DAVID: You speak English very well.

SERGIEV: I'm sorry, I don't understand.

DAVID: Your command of our language is excellent.

SERGIEV: Oh, English. My English I learn myself. I teach myself from the filthy American sexy magazines smuggled into my country back in the Seventies.

DAVID: Ah! *(They laugh good-naturedly.)* So what are your plans for the future?

SERGIEV: I plan to insert myself in your country and grow to my full, throbbing size as a novelist.

DAVID: So are you going to make your home here in London?

SERGIEV: Oh, yes. I hope your government will spread their white,

welcoming thighs and accept me with a small scream of pleasure.

DAVID: And you intend to go on writing about the pre-*perestroika* oppression of the Soviet system?

SERGIEV: Yes. I must rhythmically thrust myself into my new book. It's all about the Stalin enemas.

DAVID: The purges of the Thirties?

SERGIEV: Oh, yes. Oh, yes, Oh, yes, oh, yes. Please, please, faster.

DAVID: Are you worried about reprisals from the more reactionary elements in your country?

SERGIEV: Yes. My fear is so big, you can hardly get your hand around it. I am moist and quivering with anticipation. At this very moment the KGB could be caressing their way towards me, ready to take me unawares on the kitchen table.

MARTIN: Well, you're safe here, Sergiev.

SERGIEV: Well, I reach the plateau of ecstasy you should say so.

(*A white-coated waiter approaches with a wine bottle.*)

WAITER: Another drink, sir?

SERGIEV: Yes. Give it to me. I need to lubricate myself freely. Smear some in.

(*There is a kerfuffle. The waiter stabs Sergiev and flees. Sergiev staggers.*)

SERGIEV: Stop that waiter! He is a KGB agent! He has stabbed me with his meat dagger!

MARTIN: Sergiev, are you all right?

SERGIEV: No, no. I am throbbing and subsiding and going limp. Everything is going dank and musky. Goodbye, Big Boy.

(*Sergiev dies.*)

MARTIN: He's dead. His first novel in English was destined to become a classic. It combined Eastern mysticism with European metaphysics.

DAVID: Really? What was it called?

MARTIN: *Emmanuelle Kant Goes to Bangkok.*

I like to tease my plants when I water them. I water them with icecubes.

I like to skate on the other side of the ice.

I like to reminisce with people I don't know.

I like to fill my tub up with water and then turn the shower on and act like I'm in a submarine that's been hit.
STEVEN WRIGHT

ROWAN ATKINSON, CRAIG FERGUSON, EMMA FREUD, STEPHEN FRY, HUGH LAURIE

Condom Language

STEPHEN: A major problem with AIDS continues to be the technical question of the condom. It seems strange but it is none the less true that, in an age when we are able to talk freely and unashamedly of subjects once as forbidden and taboo as pantie shields and intimate wipes, it is still difficult to be open about sheaths. That is the topic we want to discuss this evening. The condom: how to raise the subject in intimate conversation and how then to get it on without spoiling the intimate moment.

As ever, it's the form of words, it's the problem with language, that gets in the way. We have therefore contacted some of the top writers in the country to elicit their best shot at dialogues to cope with the condom-on-cock crisis, and I have invited some of my friends – and yours, I'm sure – to help read out those dialogues. Obviously, we would have enacted them, but it is so difficult to get an erection ... of a double bed organized on stage, due to the smallness of the wings; so you are going to have to wear the print frock of Dame Imagination. Ladies and gentlemen, our celebrity guest feature readers, culled from the worlds of serious drama, madrigal singing and satanic child abuse – please welcome them.

(Enter Rowan Atkinson, Craig Ferguson, Hugh Laurie and Emma Freud, dressed in formal black and looking like opera singers about to do a recital. They bear scripts and seat themselves, straight-backed, on chairs.)

Some of you, not all, will have noticed that our readers are not naked. There will be dancing on this stage later on, and for reasons of safety it is very important that our dancers do not slip on any residues or fluids. To compensate for the disappointing lack of nudity and to help you in the task of imagining, I have asked the loved ones of our four readers to supply a sort of eroto-sketch of each of them. This will help you to undress our artistes in your minds, mentally to strip them, if you like. I read verbatim.

'Rowan has a surprisingly pert bottom. His chest hair is dark and matted, with a sweet smell of pine unexpectedly emanating from it. In moments of especial intensity his toes go pink and curl inwards.'

'Craig's dark, massy physique can be dangerous in the wrong hands. The deeper hollows and crevices repay inspection for the student of insect life. What appears to be a large birthmark in the shape of a referee's whistle offers invigorating surprises. Unusually pretty knees.'

'Emma has one of the most delicious and sought-after bodies in the United Kingdom. From the fabulous beauty of her luscious hair to the perfect contours of her bottom, she is one big, shaggable mound of Venus.' We are very grateful to Emma Freud for that description.

'The sight of Hugh's body, when burnished, oiled and sprawled on a rug in front of the fire, is enough to tempt the most jaded appetite. Notable features are the rosy, come-kiss-me cheeks and the dark, damp, come-savage-me nooks, which are kept scrupulously clean at all times. Apt to over-use the teeth when excited.'

Excellent. Our four artistes are now in our imaginations, completely naked. Well, on with the readings. The first of our four authors is – and why not? – Bob Larbey, author, adapter and scriptwriter of H. E. Bates's *The Darling Buds of May*. His contribution, unfortunately, is not quite as helpful as we'd hoped.

☆

EMMA: Oh, Pop Larkin, stick this condom on yer knob, will you?
ROWAN: Oh, yes. That fits perfick.

☆

STEPHEN: Bob's busy writing the sequel, *The Super Special Lovely Buds of May*, and clearly didn't have much time for us, but it's the thought that counts. Next we were very lucky to get some dialogue

from Tom Stoppard. The scene is a fashionable bedroom in the heart of London's famous West End.

☆

CRAIG: Darling, roll it on and let's make love now.

HUGH: Strange you should say 'make', as if the act of coition were producing an artefact of some kind. The painter Giotto could draw a perfect circle freehand.

CRAIG: How is that relevant?

HUGH: Well, it's an arty fact, too. I'm sorry, loved one, but I seem to be losing rigidity.

CRAIG: Losing rigidity or gaining frigidity? There's only an 'f' in it.

HUGH: There are two 'fs' in stiffness. A fortissimo of love. I'm sorry, angel, but I can't stay firm.

CRAIG: Stay firm or 'stop 'ard'?

HUGH: Nobody likes a clever dick.

CRAIG: Nobody likes a floppy one either. Don't go soft on me now. Think happy thoughts.

HUGH: What is happiness?

CRAIG: To a Frenchman 'apeeniss is as 'apeeniss does.

HUGH: To me happiness is Felicity. There's an 'f' in Felicity.

CRAIG: There are four 'fs' in 'Frig off, arse-face.'

HUGH: Right-o.

☆

STEPHEN: Thank you, Tom Stoppard. We were also very lucky to get some dialogue from the author of the beautiful Japanese porno . . . I'm sorry, art movie, *Ai No Corrida*, or *Empire of the Senses*. Unfortunately, the script arrived in Japanese, and we haven't been able to translate it, but I think the message still comes through.

☆

(*This starts at fever pitch and grows increasingly panty and passionate.*)

HUGH: Hai to mi no takimo.

EMMA: Ai, con, aim mu shurio.

HUGH: Tahiki, no pa rita.

EMMA: O terryaki miso . . . pants.

HUGH: O, miso terryaki . . . panty-pants.

EMMA: Oh!

HUGH: Oh!!

EMMA: Oh!!!!!

HUGH: Oh!!!!!! (*Suddenly calm and clinical.*) Ha, mashato Durex Supersmooth.

EMMA: Ha, masho Durex inito.

HUGH: Weeeshama Durex makito. Oh!!!!!

EMMA: OH!!!!!! OH, OH, OH, OH, OH, OH, OH!!!!

HUGH: Thank ryuichi.

☆

STEPHEN: Sensual joy there from the Land of the Rising . . . of the Rising . . . the Land of the Rising . . . of the Rising Sun. Our final reading comes from the pen of that most enduringly popular of thriller writers, Dick Francis.

HUGH: Darling, I think I know you and love you well enough to be able to say, without embarrassment, that I am going to slip this rubber sheath over my dong, so that our love-making will be safer and securer without being less intense. That doesn't worry you, does it, dearest?

ROWAN: (*Frighteningly life-like equine whinny.*)

☆

STEPHEN: Well, there we have it. Thank you to Bob Larbey, Tom Stoppard, Ashio Morahito and Dick Francis. I would ask you all now, in your imaginations, to put the clothing back on to our four artistes. In your minds, please reclothe our readers. Thank you. Yes, well, someone has put Emma's skirt on Rowan and left Hugh without his underpants. That's better. I can still see a little of Rowan's bottom, but who's complaining? Ladies and gentlemen, thank you very much indeed.

I wear eyeglasses during the day. Yesterday I was walking down the street wearing my eye-glasses and all of a sudden the prescription ran out.   STEVEN WRIGHT

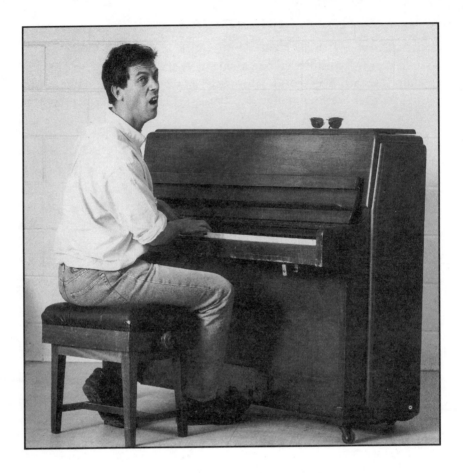

HUGH LAURIE

'Mystery'

Mystery, all my life has been a mystery.
You and I were never ever meant to be,
That's why I call my love for you a mystery.

Different country,
You and I have always lived in a different country,
And I know that airline tickets don't grow on a tree.
What kept us apart is plain for me to see,
That much at least is not really a mystery.

Estuary, I live in a house boat on an estuary,
Which is handy for my work with the Thames Water Authority,
But I know you would have found it insanitary, insanitary,

Taken a violent dislike to me.
I'd be foolish to ignore the possibility,
And if we'd ever actually met, you might have really hated me.
Still, that's not the only problem I can see.

Dead since 1973.
You've been dead now, wait a minute, let me see –
Sixteen years come next January.
As a human being you are history.

So why do I still long for you?
Why is my love so strong for you?
Why did I write this song for you?
Well, I guess it's just a mystery,
It's just a mystery . . . mystery!

HARRY ENFIELD

Sir Harry Stocracy

Hello, my loves! Ha! Ha! I feel very privileged to be invited to come along here tonight to address you all on a subject of National Importance. And the subject that I have chosen I believe to be fundamental to our very existence in the future – to whether we sink as a nation or swim, like a big, fat trout – ooh, lovely! I like a bit of trout, ooh, yes, lovely!

My subject is, of course, the importance of personal cleanliness. Now, I can see you're all thinking, why is this so important, and get on with it, and stuff like that, but it *is* important, you see, because if you're nice and clean, you feel happy, and life is full of surprises because you find yourself sitting there thinking, mmm, something smells good, and it's you, you see? Yes, ooh, yes.

Now, my programme of personal cleanliness begins every morning with my bath, which is run for me by my manservant, Mr Phillips, who fills it up – oh, yes – he fills my bath every morning with strawberry jam. This is because, when he first came into my service – ooh, must've been 5 & 20 & 3 & a half & 2 & 1 & 7 & 6 & 5 & fourpence years ago – I told him I liked strawberry jam in the morning. I meant on my toast, but he thought in my bath – it's an easy mistake to make – and I keep on forgetting to tell him that this is all a big mix-up, you know. So every morning I have this bath in strawberry jam, and it's a frightful business, it really is. It's so sticky, and you can't wallow properly. Getting the soap to lather is absolutely impossible. I don't like it at all.

I try to have a quick bath, but it's so difficult to get out because I just get stuck to the bottom, you see, and I have to wait for Mr Phillips to come and rescue me, lever me out with a spade. Fortunately,

I don't have to wait long, usually just four or five hours or something, you know, and then Mr Phillips appears with my lunch. He brings it to me in the bathroom because he knows I'll be there – he's got a seventh sense like that, he really has. But he always forgets to bring the spade up with him, so he has to leave my lunch on the side. I don't have a very big lunch, just a little snack, you now, a couple of fatted calves or something, and then he goes downstairs to get the spade to get me out. But his memory isn't all it was, poor chap, since he got knocked over by a motorbike a few years ago on his 107th birthday, so when he gets downstairs he forgets what he went down there for and carries on with his daily chores.

Ooh, there's lots of chores to be done around my house, there really is. It's never-ending. There's always puppies to be christened, dwarves to be watered, spiders that need their legs pulling off – oh, it's never-ending. D'you know, I've always wondered about this last one. I've asked Mr Phillips if the spiders really need their legs pulled off. They always look perfectly happy with all their legs to me. But apparently they love it! It's the fun of the chase and the thrill of not knowing how many legs you're going to have pulled off or whether you're going to be squashed or not that they find such fun, these spiders, according to Mr Phillips.

Anyway, the last of Mr Phillips's daily chores is, of course, digging his grave. He hasn't got long to go now. He's pretty old. He's dug himself a nice little hole at the bottom of the garden, next to the ice-cream plantation. He's nearly finished it – he's only got a couple of feet to go – and, of course, for this he uses the spade. And it's then he remembers that the spade is what I need to help me get out of the bath, so he puts off his grave-digging for a couple of minutes and comes and levers me out of the bath.

Well, after my bath I usually have a shower to get rid of all the strawberry jam. This is very important. If I forget the shower, I have a frightful time trying to get my clothes on. They get so sticky. And then I become very attractive to flies, and they swarm all over me. I can't see anything. So I try to remember my shower if I can, and after I've had my shower I'm nice and clean.

Then it's usually time . . . er . . . for bed, but before I go to bed I have my evening bath. Not in the same bathroom as I have my morning bath – that's still full of strawberry jam. No, no, I wouldn't get back in there. That would be absolute madness. No, no, I have my evening bath in the other bathroom in the west wing.

Now, Mr Phillips, who's my manservant, he's been in my household a long time now. But he's getting a bit old and forgetful, and he always forgets to run my evening bath. There's never anything in it. Well, I'm in and out of that bath pretty quickly, I can tell you. I don't lie there wallowing for hours. No, no, I don't even bother to wash, not with a bar of soap. How can you do that with a bar of soap and no water? That would be ridiculous. No, no, I only wash without water when there is no soap either: that is the only time. Yes, oh, yes. And then I go to bed. Goodnight.

Whenever I pick up someone hitchhiking I always like to wait a few minutes before I say anything to them. Then I say, 'So, how far did you think you were going? Put your seatbelt on – I wanna try something. I saw it in a cartoon, but I'm pretty sure I can do it.'

If you shoot a mime, should you use a silencer?
STEVEN WRIGHT

STEPHEN FRY AND HUGH LAURIE

Masterclass

SF: Hello, good evening and welcome to a frighteningly special edition of piano masterclass, and we're very lucky to have with us this evening young Hugh. Hello, Hugh.

HL: Hi!

SF: Excellent, well done. Very good, very, very good. Right, so have you chosen a piece of music for us?

HL: Yes, I've chosen Shelper's 'Bridal Nocturne'.

SF: Shelper's 'Bridal Nocturne'. All right, OK, would you like to go and sit down then? You've got your music? There's the piano. (*Hugh goes and sits at piano.*) Hugh, Hugh. What do you think you're doing?

HL: Well, you told me to sit down.

SF: Yes. Hitch, hitch, hitch.

HL: I beg your pardon?

SF: Hitch your trousers, Hugh. Hitch your trousers. You're not loose at the knee. If you're not loose at the knee, you might as well not be here.

HL: Oh, all right. (*He starts to walk off the stage.*)

SF: No, Hugh, come back, come back. I can help you to go nice and loose at the knee . . . relaxed and fluent. (*Stephen hits him on the back of the knee. Hugh falls.*) All right? That's good . . . Now go and do that over the stool.

HL: (*Sits again.*) OK.

SF: Lovely. All right. Now, open the piano.

HL: (*Tries but can't.*) It's locked.

SF: What?

HL: The lid is locked.

SF: Um . . . shit. Not to worry. Look around you, improvise. What do you see?

HL: A locked piano.

SF: Look, here's a guitar. Use this.

HL: I can't play the guitar.

SF: No, use it to smash open the piano.

HL: Oh, right. (*He does so.*)

SF: Excellent. Well done. Now, Hugh, are your hands nice and warm?

HL: Well, they could be warmer.

sf: All right, well, we'll warm them up then. It's very important not to have any stiffness.

hl: No.

sf: All right, so here's an old trick to help you warm your hands. Put them between the legs, like that, and give them a good warm-up. (*Stephen puts his hands between his legs and rubs them together hard.*)

hl: OK.

sf: Try that now. (*Hugh puts his hands between Stephen's legs and rubs them together.*) No, no, your own legs.

hl: Oh, sorry.

sf: We don't want any stiffness. That's it, nice and warmed-up and relaxed?

hl: Yes, I think so.

sf: Fluent at the knee?

hl: Yes.

sf: All right then. Now, what's the time signature of your piece?

hl: Um, 3/4.

sf: Now, that's a waltz time, isn't it?

hl: Yes.

sf: What's the key thing about waltzes, Hugh?

hl: They're in 3/4 time.

sf: They're frothy, they're giddy, they're romantic, they're light. So let's see a frothy, giddy, light, romantic attitude to the keyboard, all right? Ha ha ha ha.

hl: Ha ha ha ha.

sf: Ha ha ha ha ha ha.

hl: Ha ha ha ha ha ha ha ha.

sf: Yes, not too frothy, Hugh. We can't afford to be too frothy. Now, cock nice and high. (*Hugh positions his hands in the air.*) Cock higher. Cock as high as you can. That's lovely. All right . . . *and* one, two, three, one, two, three, and down down, and down down, and down down, and . . .

hl: (*Still sitting with hands in the air.*) Shall I start?

sf: Yes, go. Go on, yes.

hl: (*Plays.*)

sf: Yes, all right, woah, woah, woah, Hugh. This is a bridal nocturne, isn't it?

HL: Yes.

SF: Bridal nocturne. Do you have a girlfriend, Hugh?

HL: Yes, I have, as a matter of fact.

SF: Do you make love on a regular basis?

HL: Well, you know . . .

SF: Did you make love last night?

HL: Um.

SF: You don't have to answer that.

HL: Oh, right.

SF: Well?

HL: Well, what?

SF: Did you make love last night?

HL: Well, yes, I did as a matter of fact. Yes.

SF: All right, I want you to relive that experience in your mind, all right? Are you making love again in your mind as you did last night?

HL: Nearly.

SF: Good. All right, now I want you to play for me exactly as you made love last night.

HL: Right. (*Plays much faster but not for very long. Ends suddenly.*)

SF: That's it, is it?

HL: Well, yes. I'm sorry. It's not your fault. I'm tired.

SF: OK, not to worry, not to worry. If you'd just like to shift over there and lose your stiffness, I'll show you how it should be done, all right? (*Stephen pushes Hugh off the stool and sits down himself.*) Cock high, relaxed at the knees, frothy, all right? Yes? (*Stephen plays a load of garbage.*) You see?

HL: Yes, um . . .

SF: Yes, what?

HL: No, nothing, nothing.

SF: No, go on.

HL: Well, it wasn't very good, was it?

SF: Uh?

HL: Well, I mean, you didn't play it very well.

SF: Yes, well, that's all we have time for this evening . . .

HL: In fact, it really was . . . That was enormously bad.

SF: Yes, yes, that's all we have time for this evening . . .

HL: How long have you been teaching the piano?

SF: I teach pupils, Hugh. I don't teach the piano. That would be stupid. It's just a lump of wood . . . If you're so clever, play this, sight-read this. This shit-hot student is going to play for you now, sight-reading.

HL: What is it? What is it?

SF: Never you mind what it is. Just play it. (*Hugh plays final cadence.*) Thank you.

CLIVE ANDERSON

This is an exciting time to be performing, isn't it? Of course, I'm very excited about deciding which of the ten water and sewerage businesses of England and Wales to put my money into.

I'd like to join in on a theme that some other performers have been developing on the environment. I'm a big fan of the environment myself. After all, I live there. And I'm very pleased that a lot of people have turned . . . Even Margaret Thatcher has turned green, hasn't she? Probably as a result of swimming in the North Sea. It turns out there are more chemicals in the North Sea than in a sample of Ben Johnson's urine. There are a lot of resorts around the British Isles. You can't go for a swim any more, not really. All you can do is to get in the water and go through the motions.

But it's all these dreadful things like oil disasters that seem to go on the whole time. Nothing quite as bad yet here as that dreadful one, the Exxon disaster in Alaska, but I've got a friend in oil . . . He's in oil in a small way. In fact, he's a sardine. No, obviously he's not. Obviously he's not. No, that's a silly joke. Sorry, sorry. He's a pilchard. Apparently, according to him, the Esso companies, as they used to be called, changed their name to Exxon some time ago because the word 'Esso' was a rude word in Japanese or something like that, but unfortunately now Exxon is a rude word in Alaska. The Eskimos in Alaska apparently have got fourteen different words for snow, and now they've got twenty-seven words for oil slick. And they all begin with 'f' and they end in '-king Exxon'.

BILLY BRAGG BAND

'Sexuality'

I've had relations with girls from many nations.
I've made passes at women of all classes.
And just because you're gay,
I won't turn you away.
If you stick around,
I'm sure that we can find some common ground.

Sexuality:
Strong and warm and wild and free.
Sexuality:
Your laws do not apply to me.

A nuclear submarine sinks off the coast of Sweden.
Headlines give me headaches when I read them.
I had an uncle who once played
For Red Star, Belgrade.
He said that some things are really best left unspoken,
But I'd prefer it all to be out in the open.

Sexuality:
Young and warm and wild and free.
Sexuality:
Your laws do not apply to me.
Sexuality:
Don't threaten me with misery.
Sexuality:
I demand equality.

I'm sure that everybody knows how much my body hates me.
It lets me down most every time and makes me rash and hasty.
I feel a total jerk
Before your naked body of work.

I'm getting weighed down
With all this information.
Safe sex doesn't mean no sex:
It just means use your imagination.

Stop playing with yourselves
In hard-currency hotels.
I look like Robert De Niro.
I drive a Mitsubishi Zero.

Sexuality:
Strong and warm and wild and free.
Sexuality:
Your laws do not apply to me.
Sexuality:
Come eat and drink and sleep with me.
Sexuality:
We can be what we want to be.
Sexuality.

HUGH LAURIE

Army Officer

Ladies and gentlemen, as I'm sure you're aware, there's been over the last few weeks a great deal of nonsense spoken in the newspapers and written on the television about the issue of homosexuality in Her Majesty's Armed Forces, or HMAF, as we call them for short, or FSH as we call . . . Anyway, there are just a couple of points I'd like to make. The question, it seems to me, is does homosexuality, as a way of life, or even just as a hobby, diminish the fighting efficiency of a military organization, which is essentially what the British Army is in the business of being?

Now, I should make clear first of all that I myself have nothing against homosexuality in principle. My concern is whether or not it actually works in practice. I have always taken the view that if God had intended men to be homosexual, he would have issued them with more attractively shaped bottoms.

However, I should point out that I have known several homosexuals quite well – in fact, I used to go to bed with a young Turkish boy called Abul when I was stationed in Cyprus. Most obliging lad . . . But anyway he, it later turned out, was, in fact, homosexual. I had to stop seeing him once I'd found out, naturally. But I raise this in order to show that I have nothing personally against homosexual men. I wouldn't want my daughter to marry one, perhaps, but that is another matter.

However, I must confess to very severe misgivings when I hear the idea being mooted, and it is being mooted, possibly over-mooted, that our national defence be placed in the hands of gaysexuals of any description. The fact is that your modern homosexual is a highly trained, highly motivated individual, capable, if he or she so chooses, of resembling an ordinary person at a moment's notice. Precisely. Chilling thought. You take a handful of these dedicated chutney ferrets, place them in the midst of a modern British fighting unit and they are going to have a bloody field day.

Let us imagine, for the sake of argument, the pilot and navigator of a Tornado ground-attack aircraft flying a dangerous mission into enemy territory. Two young men, far from home, thrown into very cramped and uncomfortable surroundings. Suddenly, and without warning, they are fired upon by enemy aircraft. With only seconds in which to avoid the impact of an air-to-air missile, the pilot removes his hands from the controls, turns round in the cockpit and begins to make sexual advances towards his navigator. Strategically speaking, this would be the worst possible course of action. Instead of getting their heads down and flying the aeroplane . . . Well, instead of flying the aeroplane, they would be getting their heads down. An extremely valuable piece of military kit would be put at risk, and a thoroughly bad example shown to anyone who happened to be listening on the radio. That way, quite obviously, madness lies.

But let us imagine an even more alarming possibility, what I call the absolute nightmare scenario. A young infantryman, called Jimmy – for he may very easily be Scottish – comes face to face with his Arab foe under the fierce desert sun. But, instead of shooting his enemy dead, Jimmy throws his rifle to one side and, in halting Arabic, suggests that the two of them repair to a nearby motel bedroom. Instead of engaging the enemy Jimmy has become engaged to the enemy. Once again, chaos. I can only say that if you study your military history closely enough, you will see that no war has ever been won by going to bed with your opponent. It simply does not make military sense.

Now, of course, there are those who say that in its attitude to homosexuality the British Army is being hidebound. Take the Foreign Office, they will say. It is well known that there are one or two heterosexuals in the Foreign Office . . . I'm sorry, one or two homosexuals . . . No, I'm sorry, one or two heterosexuals . . . in the Foreign Office, and that, after all, seems to function pretty well most of the time. To them I would say, when it comes to the defence of our country 'pretty well most of the time' is a long way short of being good enough. The idea that the flower of British youth, instead of getting out there and killing people in the most cost-efficient manner possible, should simply spend its time going to bed with itself just does not bear thinking about.

I was in bed with my girlfriend reading this second-hand diary that I bought.

She said, 'Let me ask you this.'
I said, 'What?'
She said, 'If you could know how and when you were gonna die, would you wanna know?'
I said, 'No.'
She said, 'Forget it then.'

I figured I'd get up and go for a walk. She said, 'How long are you going to be gone?'
I said, 'The whole time.' STEVEN WRIGHT

Sex Counsellor

SF: Send in the next one, Mrs Frittle-P-Postlecreelpiss. (*Enter Lenny.*) Well, good afternoon Mr . . . er . . . Mr . . . er.

LH: Wildebeeste, Theopolis P. Wildebeeste. (*Sings*) 'Soul singer.'

. SF: And how may I help, Mr Wildebeeste?

LH: Well, er, mind if I sit? Because I have to get myself in place. Jingle my things around. Are you the main homeboys' sex-counsellor dude in this town?

SF: Well, I am a sex counsellor, certainly, yes.

LH: Well, baby . . . I can call you 'baby', can I?

SF: If it gives you pleasure.

LH: Well, baby, the thing is, I need some advice. You see, I've got a big, big drive. I think you know what I'm talking about.

SF: I see. Is this . . . um . . . gravel or tarmac?

LH: Say what?

SF: This drive of yours, is it gravel or is it tarmac?

LH: No, no, no. I'm talking about the *loooove* drive.

SF: Ah. You mean you have a powerful libido?

LH: Libido, bullshit. I got an Eldorado with, like, a jacuzzi, a targa roof and twin carburettors.

SF: I mean, you have strong sex urges?

LH: Hey, that's right, baby, urges. When I urges, I surges. I think you know what I'm talking about.

SF: Yes, I'm rather afraid I do. And your trouble is that you can't find any partners. Is that it?

LH: Hey, hey, do you know who you're talking to here? I'm the guy the chicks die for.

SF: So you're some sort of poultry farmer, is that it?

LH: Listen, asshole . . .

SF: I think I prefer 'baby'.

LH: I can get it whenever I want it, awright? I just feel deep within my heart, within my soul, deep down within the core of my being, within my *chi*, that I need to be a little more careful, you dig?

SF: Ah, you're interested in safer sex.

LH: Hey, now you're locking into the socket. Now you're right in the groove, brother.

SF: Good, good. You're interested in ways of practising . . .

LH: Hey, lover, I don't need no practice, awright?

SF: I'm sorry.

LH: I just need to find the right way to take care of my ass and shit.

SF: You want to take care of your arse and shit?

LH: Bang it on.

SF: I see.

LH: I'm aiming to be a responsible citizen, you know what I'm talking about?

SF: Well, about one word in twenty seems to be making sense, yes.

LH: (*Laughs.*) I like you, baby. I like your white ass.

SF: Thank you. It is rather stylish, isn't it?

LH: Right.

SF: Well, the most simple, straightforward and effective way of practising . . . performing straight sex is to wear a condom.

LH: Condom?

SF: Yes.

LH: Oh, a 'carndom'.

SF: That's right.

LH: The thing is, baby, I've seen these condoms, right, and the thing is, the truth of the matter is, you see, I'm not the kind of guy to beat about the bush. You know what I'm talking about?

SF: I hope I don't.

LH: The thing is, they're too small.

SF: The condoms are too small?

LH: They're too small. I can barely get them over my ears.

SF: Yes . . . um . . . the basic principle behind them, Mr Wildebeeste, is to put them on your . . . as you would say, your dick.

LH: On my dick?

SF: Yes.

LH: Woooow! On my dick. What happens then?

SF: Well, then you and your partner are protected from infection.

LH: How's that?

SF: Well, the condom will collect your seminal fluid.

LH: Oh, right. (*Sings*) 'Ain't no stopping us now.' Give me five.

SF: All right. Five condoms. What size?

LH: Hey, you have to ask?

SF: No, of course not, I'm sorry. Five condoms, small. There you are.

LH: Right. And let me have a bottle of that seminal fluid too.

CHRIS LYNAM

Ladies and gentlemen, I don't believe I'm going to do this next sketch, but, yes, it's true. We've been racking our brains all day to find a safe-sex link for it. Couldn't find one.

And so if you find a safe-sex link for this next sketch, could you write to your MPs? I'd like just to dedicate this next piece to all the comedians who've ever worked in the world up to now – Grimaldi, Buster Keaton, Charlie Chaplin, Margaret Thatcher.

I'm going to stick a firework up my arse and light it. It's true.

(Chris Lynam sticks a large firework up his arse and lights it to the music of 'That's Entertainment'.)

The Hedge Sketch

STEPHEN: Ladies and gentlemen, we'd like to do a sketch for you now. It's set in a shop, and it's called the Hedge Sketch. The Hedge Sketch. Thank you very much indeed.

(*Stephen stands at a small shop counter. Enter Hugh.*)

HUGH: Hello. I'd like to buy a hedge.

STEPHEN: Good morning, sir. How may I help you?

HUGH: Well, what sorts have you got?

STEPHEN: A hedge? What sort of hedge would you like?

HUGH: Could I have a look at the Imperial?

STEPHEN: Well, we have three sorts, sir. The Royal, the Imperial and the Standard hedge.

HUGH: No, it's a present.

STEPHEN: Certainly. May I ask, is the hedge for you?

HUGH: I'm not married.

STEPHEN: For your wife perhaps?

HUGH: Not at all. I'm in no hurry.

STEPHEN: Splendid. I'll just ring down if you wouldn't mind waiting?

HUGH: (*Whispers*) Start again. Start again.

STEPHEN: Right.

(*They turn away, mutter and start again.*)

STEPHEN: Good morning, sir. How may I help you?

HUGH: Hello. I'd like to buy a hedge.

STEPHEN: A hedge? What sort of hedge would you like?

HUGH: Well, we have three sorts, sir. The Royal, the Imperial, or the Standard hedge.

(*Pause.*)

STEPHEN: Could I have a look at the Imperial?
HUGH: Certainly. May I ask, is the hedge for you?
STEPHEN: No, it's a present.
HUGH: For your wife perhaps?
STEPHEN: I'm not married.
HUGH: Splendid. I'll just ring down if you wouldn't mind waiting?
STEPHEN: Not at all. I'm in no hurry.

(*Hugh goes behind the counter. He can't find the telephone.*)

HUGH: (*Whispers*) There's no telephone!
STEPHEN: Under the counter.
HUGH: Where?
STEPHEN: I'll do it.
HUGH: No, I'll do it. (*Picks up phone.*) Hello, stockroom? Have we got any Imperial hedges left?

(*Pause.*)

STEPHEN: (*Gamely pretending to be the phone*) I'll just have a look, sir.
HUGH: Thanks. (*To Stephen*) He's just checking.
STEPHEN: We've got one left.
HUGH: Right, I'll take it then.

(*Hugh puts down the phone and goes round to the other side of the counter. Stephen picks up the phone and puts it down again.*)

STEPHEN: You seem to be in luck, sir. Stockroom tells me that we've got one Imperial left.
HUGH: (*Pause*) Cash, if you don't mind.
STEPHEN: How would you like to pay, sir?
HUGH: Start again?
STEPHEN: Definitely. (*Sets off incredibly fast*) Good morning, sir. How can I help you?
HUGH: Hello. I'd like to buy a hedge.
STEPHEN: Certainly. What sort of hedge would you like?
HUGH: Well, what sorts have you got?

STEPHEN: Well, we have three sorts, sir. The Royal, the Imperial and the Standard hedge.

HUGH: Could I have a look at the Imperial?

STEPHEN: Certainly, sir. May I ask, is the hedge for you?

HUGH: No, it's a present.

STEPHEN: For your wife perhaps?

HUGH: I'm not married.

STEPHEN: Splendid. I'll just ring down if you wouldn't mind waiting?

HUGH: Not at all. I'm in no hurry.

STEPHEN: Hello, stockroom ... (*Hugh gestures at the telephone. Stephen picks it up.*) Hello, stockroom. Have we got any Imperial hedges left? He's-just-checking-you're-in-luck-sir-we've-got-one-left.

HUGH: Right, I'll take it then.

STEPHEN: How would you like to pay, sir?

HUGH: Certainly, sir. Cash would be perfectly convenient.

BOTH: Right.

(*There follows a colossal pause. Lights dim down.*)

Y*ou know the pyjamas with the feet? I just had the feet.*

Y*ou know when you put a stick in the water and it looks like it's bent but it really isn't? That's why I don't take baths.*   STEVEN WRIGHT

STEPHEN FRY

Goodnight

Ladies and gentlemen, you have been patient, pure and kind beyond imagining. You know, there are those who have written and said over the last few years that evenings like this are nothing more than the outpourings of a trendy liberal conscience, that AIDS is an exaggerated problem, confined only to the weirder and freakier margins of society. A right-wing economist was extensively quoted in the press only a few weeks ago as having written that the 'gay community' – the printer couldn't provide quotation marks big enough for him to show his distaste for the phrase – has a vested interest in, indeed desperately wants, the virus to spread to the rest of the population so that their hysterical reactions could be justified.

The sickness of this economist is spreading the disease, I am sorry to say. This attitude – an attitude denied and, indeed, positively refuted by the medical profession, the government's own health officers and the experience of other countries – this attitude that somehow AIDS is a problem only for the deviant few, this attitude is the trendy one. It is a trend that has to be bucked. Trendy right-wing economists and trendy journalists can be assured that the greatest wish in the world of everyone working in and around the problems of HIV is that they will be proved wrong, that AIDS will fizzle out as a problem, that it will somehow go away instead of spreading across the world and across society.

Everyone deeply hopes that this will be the case. We also hope that we can all eat as much as we like without getting fat. We hope that we can step out of the window and float through the air. We hope that, by closing our eyes tightly and wishing, starvation, cruelty, ignorance, shiny-shell tracksuits and the programme *Telly Addicts* will simply disappear. We can hope all these things, but when the evidence of experience and research shows that none of these hopes is ever likely to be fulfilled, surely the best thing to do is to help those who are being struck down by this dreadful pestilence.

It cannot be said enough that if AIDS were to last a thousand years, it will not have provided so grisly a toll of hardship, pain and misery as that provided by the real killer of mankind's hopes: bigotry.

The money that this show has raised, and will continue to raise through video, book, television and album sales, goes directly to help those living with AIDS. It goes to hospices for those with AIDS and to Britain's oldest AIDS charity, the Terrence Higgins Trust. They are eternally grateful to you, as I am and as are all the performers who have given up their time to be here today.

We salute you. We metaphorically stroke your proud, shining flanks. We figuratively prod, poke and paddle your yielding flesh, tousling your hair in a profoundly sensitive and caring fashion. In a manner of speaking, we shag you senseless. Thank you all so very, very much.

HAT TRICK PRODUCTIONS LTD

Dear Stephen,

As requested, I have kept July as free as possible for the Hysteria Show. But now I am gob-smacked (as government ministers would put it) to learn that Hysteria 3 is to take place not in July at all, but on June 30th. Is this some fogeyish affectation: sticking to pounds, shillings and pence, and the Julian calendar? Or has your occasional brush with the world of advertising corrupted your standards sufficiently for you to be to content to assert, albeit indirectly, that June 30th is indeed part of July?

This is not mere pedantry. It is pedantry combined with bluster to cover my embarrassment that on June 30th I am unable to be at the Palladium. I shall not even be in England.

Of course the show must go on. Continue, if you must, to suggest that I am going to take part. But risk the anger of the mob when it is announced that some poor substitute such as Griff Rhys Jones or Madonna is to take my place. Better still let Hysteria own up to the fact that I will not be performing that evening. My absence from West End shows is often a great selling point. Take Cats and Les Miserables, for example.

Anyway, I am sorry I shall not be able to be there, but I hope and I am sure the evening will be a great success.

Yours sincerely,

Clive Anderson.

Dawn French

Dear Mr. fry

Thank you for your letter.

I would be delighted to take part in
HYSTERIA, Hollywood contracts permitting.

However, I could only conceivably contribute
if you would kindly note the following.
Below is a list of comedians I have
slept with. I therefore do not wish to
appear with them on stage.

1. Ronald Atkinson
2. Hugh Laurie
3. Hale and Pace
4. Hugh Laurie
5. Jennifer Saunders
6. Hugh Laurie
7. The Prince of Wales

I do hope you understand.

I look forward to hearing from you.

With best wishes.

Yours sincerely

POOPOOPICTURES

Dear Stephen,

March 25,1991

O.K. you got me! As you may or may not know, I've always had a soft spot for plagues. And, as you say, AIDS is the big one. To be fair there have been bigger ones but, this is the best we've got - so we better make the most of it.

As you also may or may not know, the thought of me getting up on stage and trying to be funny fills me with dread. Unless I have an exploding stomach or a hat full of vomit or several custard pies or indescribeably thick make-up to hide behind I don't enjoy the experience... and, furthermore, I'm trying desperately hard to get my children to recognise me as a serious film maker. I'm sure you can understand the difficulty of my situation.

However, you offer the possibility of working in some combination with others that has never occurred to me. Perhaps this is the solution. But, how will this new combination reveal itself? How will I recognise it? Will it be legal? Do we have to do it in public? Will we catch AIDS doing it? This sounds like an even more difficult situation than the one with which we ended the previous paragraph.

Can I leave the sorting out of the details with you? Remember, if all else fails, I can still draw.

Yours in good health,

Terry (Gilliam)

From the Office of

J. M. Holland

2nd April 1991

Dear Stephen

Thank you so much for your kind letter. I was overcome with emotion and nostalgic memories of the times we spent together, moments that brought a glimmer of light into my otherwise grey and drab life.

How can I ever repay what you have done for me?. I used to be Mr. Blue Skies Misery Piss, now I hold my head up high, proud to be young, proud to have hair, grateful I know you.

In short, I am happy and honoured to help you with your charity for the orphans 25 hours a day, 8 days a week, 2 weeks a year. Not only do I offer my own services, but also tentatively offer the services of my 17 piece dance orchestra, the phenomena consisting of 4 trumpets, 4 trombones, 5 saxaphones and a rhythm section known as 'Jools Holland and the Deptford Dance Orchestra'.

Always,

FRANKIE HOWERD O.B.E.

Mr. Stephen Fry,
HYSTERIA,
2, Newburgh Street,
London, W.1.V 1LH.

9th August, 1989.

Dear All,

In the first place I was meant to be with you tonight, but then they changed the place of the Show and the date which made it very difficult for me because if it had been held as it was going to be in the first place, I could, as I said in the first place, have been with you but as the first place was changed to the second place I found that I could not be with you in the second place which is here tonight, as I had contracted to do another show in the first place which is of course in another place, so in other words I am not only somewhere else but performing at this very moment.

To sum up, I must admit that I am rather sorry I started writing this letter in the first place, and for the second place I am quite sure you are sorry you started reading it. Nevertheless, I would like to place it on record - whatever your place in life - I wish you the very best.

Succintly,

FRANKIE HOWERD

P.S. I bet you are rather glad that I am performing in this second place - you have had a lucky escape !

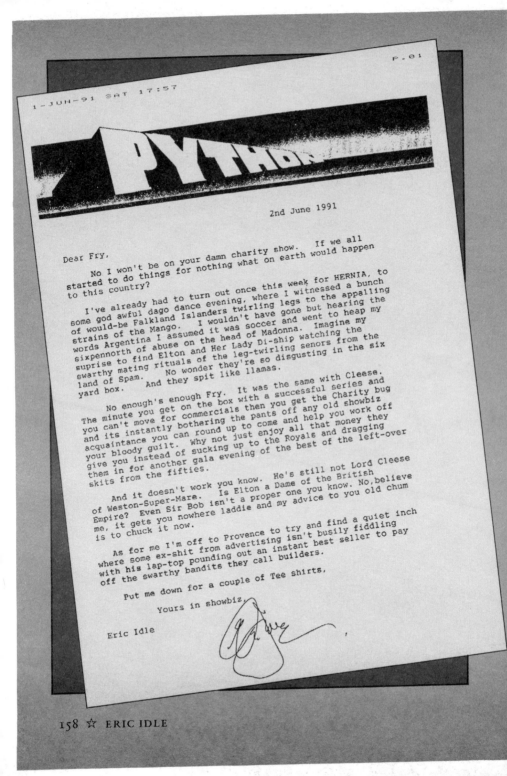

PYTHON

2nd June 1991

Dear Fry,

No I won't be on your damn charity show.   If we all started to do things for nothing what on earth would happen to this country?

I've already had to turn out once this week for HERNIA, to some god awful dago dance evening, where I witnessed a bunch of would-be Falkland Islanders twirling legs to the appalling strains of the Mango.   I wouldn't have gone but hearing the words Argentina I assumed it was soccer and went to heap my sixpennorth of abuse on the head of Madonna. Imagine my suprise to find Elton and Her Lady Di-ship watching the swarthy mating rituals of the leg-twirling senors from the land of Spam.   No wonder they're so disgusting in the six yard box.   And they spit like llamas.

No enough's enough Fry. It was the same with Cleese. The minute you get on the box with a successful series and you can't move for commercials then you get the Charity bug and its instantly bothering the pants off any old showbiz acquaintance you can round up to come and help you work off your bloody guilt. Why not just enjoy all that money they give you instead of sucking up to the Royals and dragging them in for another gala evening of the best of the left-over skits from the fifties.

And it doesn't work you know. He's still not Lord Cleese of Weston-Super-Mare. Is Elton a Dame of the British Empire? Even Sir Bob isn't a proper one you know. No,believe me, it gets you nowhere laddie and my advice to you old chum is to chuck it now.

As for me I'm off to Provence to try and find a quiet inch where some ex-shit from advertising isn't busily fiddling with his lap-top pounding out an instant best seller to pay off the swarthy bandits they call builders.

Put me down for a couple of Tee shirts,

Yours in showbiz,

Eric Idle

PYTHON

30th May, 1991

Dear Stephen —

Life is such a bitch!   There I was, tingling with excitement
at the prospect of lining up with you all on the Palladium
stage on June 30th when along came this bloody offer to do a
film role with Madonna, Woody Allen and Michelle Pfeiffer in
some wretched West Indian island - on that very same evening!
I rang my agent straight away but she wasn't in so now I've
got to <u>do</u> it!   I'm livid, because although multi-million
dollar Hollywood roles can cheer up the bank manager, they
are in no way, repeat <u>no</u> way a substitute for that visceral
rush of raw excitement that is the HYSTERIA audience.
Believe me there is only one place I want to be on June 30th
and unless I'm on the beach or having a massage, I'll be
thinking of you.

Good luck,

Michael.

voice at the end of the phone was harsh and stentorious. 'If you don't get the piece done by tonight, Mr Fry, we'll just have to cancel our agreement to print the book.'

Stephen 'Lawks' Fry, the big-boned gagsmith, fell back on to his red couch in despair. He'd organized the whole benefit so well, and now, just at the last hurdle, it looked like he was going to fall. 'Lawks,' he exclaimed, in a way which would have made them roar with laughter on the very popular *Saturday Night Live with Ben Elton Show*. 'If there's no last page, there's no book. What am I to do?!!!!!'

Suddenly he had a brainwave. He reached for his phone and dialled quickly. 'Hello,' said a fuzzy answerphone. 'This is Mel "Rhymes With Smell" Smith here. I'm afraid I'm not in at the moment, but if you'd like to wait a couple of years, my sort of humour is bound to come back into fashion. Thank you.'

Great gag, Mel, thought Stephen: but it wasn't any use to him. 'Lawks!!' he exclaimed once more, but this time with a tinge of unwonted sadness, and went into the bathroom. There stood the bottle of arsenic he'd once bought to poison Ben Elton. He imagined the headline next day: 'Stephen "Lawks" Fry Dies in Arsenic Horror – Benefit Book Cancelled'.

Ten minutes later Stephen lay on the couch, staring at the glass, now full of arsenic. Then an idea hit him. 'Lawks!!' he exclaimed. 'Why not write the last page of the book like the last page of a novel in which someone kills himself because he can't think of the last page of a book!?'

He rushed to his desk, sat down and started writing. 'The voice at the end of the phone was harsh and stentorious.' But no – wait!!! It must look like a page turned over, he thought. He re-started: 'voice at the end of the phone was harsh and stentorious'. This was more like it – he took an enthusiastic swig of the glass he held in his hand. 'Lawks!!!!!!!!!!' he exclaimed loudly, and for the last time.

A headline did indeed appear in the paper next day. It read 'Friend of Mel Smith Dies in Obscurity'. Beneath it was an article about an extremely successful benefit concert the night before. Particular praise was lavished on the book of the show, and most especially the very amusing blank page at the end.